WITHDRAWN

Let's Talk of Wills

SARAH J. MASON

Let's Talk of Wills

St. Martin's Press
New York

Library of Congress Cataloging in Publication Data

Mason, Sarah J.
　Let's talk of wills.

　I. Title.
PR6063.A7648L4　1986　　　　823'.914　　　　86-13034
ISBN 0-312-48225-6　 /1-8ს

First published in Great Britain by William Collins Sons & Co. Ltd.
First U.S. Edition

10 9 8 7 6 5 4 3 2 1

Let's Talk of Wills

CHAPTER 1

Consequences, it is written, are unpitying. Our deeds carry their terrible consequences, quite apart from any fluctuations that went before—consequences that are hardly ever confined to ourselves. All for the want of the horse-shoe nail of good temper, Sampson Stockfish was the onlie begetter of the murder at Swan House—not that he would have cared much, had anyone ever tried to blame him for it, but the roundabout cause of that murder he undoubtedly was.

A cheerful disposition comes hard to one fatherless at three and abandoned by a sluttish mother at fifteen; distant relatives did their best for the wretched Sampson by adopting him into their household and finding him employment on the Keepdown estate, which they themselves served. The Swan House squires approved, ironically enough, such a fulfilment of family obligation; even though when Old Mr Keepdown died Lucian, his younger son, succeeded him at once, encouraged by his wife to ignore completely any moral claim upon the inheritance from the widow and child of his elder brother. Young Mrs Luke thus became Mrs Squire Keepdown, and upon her husband's demise assumed complete control over the manor, its estate, and its staff.

Stockfish was for a time a problem. Born misogynists, confirmed in their prejudice by life's harsh treatment, do not take kindly to the sudden and monstrous regiment of women after years of masculine dominion. It grated upon the gardener-cum-handyman that Kate Keepdown had been the ruling power in the manor house (or at least in Mr Luke's part of it) since her days as a youthful bride, returning from a romantic elopement: he kept an ever-wary eye open for her secret approaches, and prepared well in advance arguments to counter her slightest suggestion.

It is not surprising that, with two such strong-minded persons, a mutually hostile respect grew up over the years: they came soon to welcome their periodic disputes as en-livening an otherwise routine existence, and eventually (though each would rather have suffered torments than admit it), had to acknowledge that they positively relished every vociferous encounter—neither giving way to the other, honour satisfied, and a sparkle added to the rest of the week in anticipation of the next affray.

But, on the occasion which must be seen as the true beginning of the end, Kate for once goaded Stockfish too far. Intent upon criticizing whatever, in his capacity as gardener, he'd planned to do about the daisies on the lawn —if he wanted to grub them up, she'd insist that they stayed; if he showed the least inclination to save himself bother by praising their scattered prettiness, she'd demand their instant and total elimination—she came stumping along the gravel path, emphatically waving her swagger-stick. The Allshire Regiment, in which Lucian Keepdown had briefly served as an officer, is like no other in England, for it boasts, instead of a short ornamental cane, a stick nearly three feet long, heavy with horn about a steel core, and thickly plastered to resemble whitethorn. This lethal appendage traditionally commemorates the boasted escape of General Sir John Oldcastle from a charging rhinoceros, which he claimed to have skewered with a providential swordstick— although, after two drunken regimental duellists had acci-dentally eliminated each other with their ceremonial weapons, the edict went out that the White Rhinos, as they are popularly known, must henceforth carry such a stick in name only.

Since this merely symbolic swordstick could doubtless be turned to deadly purpose in the wrong hands, it was fortu-nate for Kate that Stockfish didn't snatch it from her to reinforce his point of view. But the pruning-hook he held in an infuriated grasp served almost as well, except that he missed. Instead of his employer's proud head, he lopped off a thorny rose-stem which bore a promising shoot he'd earmarked for grafting purposes. With a frustrated bellow, he flung away his horticultural weapon; abandoning the fallen branch where, in the later evening gloom, Kate tumbled over it.

A fractured femur didn't curb her tongue. Grumbling awfully, she was loaded on a hasty litter fashioned from nets, beanpoles, and other provident articles from the potting-shed; and was carried indoors by Stockfish (never mind that she'd fired him as soon as she saw him) and the butler, Humphrey Hour, whom she cursed for every jolt and judder.

'You should've bided there till the doctor could come to you,' retorted Hour, with truth, plodding onwards.

'What! And catch my death lying on that damp grass—that's how much you think of the one who pays your wages, is it? I suppose you expect to come into a nice little bit when I go at last—but I'm not ready to go, not by a long way I'm not! Oh, I'll be around for a good while yet!'

Stockfish muttered darkly (and inaudibly), but, as they neared the house, Kate ignored both gardener and butler as she embarked upon her role as the stoic sufferer. 'Alice must scrub the table properly,' she began, almost before she'd been laid on the sofa, 'and Susan must keep plenty of hot water boiling—and you, d'you hear me, Stockfish, fetch in more logs for the stove. Make haste, do—the doctor won't want to have to wait around all night while you dally and dither about the place!'

But Dr Pickbone had no intention of waiting for anyone. Guessing from the telephone message what had happened to his wilful patient, he'd been farsighted enough to bring an ambulance with him. Two uniformed men with a red-blanketed stretcher fretted grim-faced in the hall, while Mrs Keepdown refused to listen to sound medical advice, and argued with Dr Pickbone in the sitting-room.

'Maybe it's broken—and then, maybe it isn't,' stated the old lady. 'You might pretend to know what you're talking about, I can't say—but I do know you won't get me in any hospital to be cut open and messed about! People die in hospitals, don't they? Well, I'm staying here! I've told them in the kitchen to get everything ready—'

'Kate, this is preposterous!' snapped Pickbone. 'Really, if I didn't know you so well, I'd say that the shock of the accident must have temporarily unhinged you—but all this nonsense you're talking is no more the result of a confused mind than—' He blushed, coughed, and began an embarrassed re-coiling of his already spiral stethoscope.

'Plain awkward she allus was, as a young woman,' came a stern voice from the french windows, where Alice Shortcake, cook-housekeeper of Swan House, stood propriety. 'Awkward she'll ever be, I don't doubt—but she oughter be downright ashamed of herself for causing all this fuss. If Doctor says as you should go to hospital, then go you must —and, so far as I can see, that's all there is about it.'

Mrs Keepdown glared at Mrs Shortcake; Mrs Shortcake, her arms folded, glared back, unquelled. Kate decided to vary her tactics, and turned back to the doctor: who hastily removed a broad grin from his face, and tried hard to assume a reproving, officially severe expression.

'I'm an invalid,' she announced with an artistic groan, and wriggled angrily on the sofa. 'You ought to be looking after me, not carrying on this way with no respect and no sympathy. At my age, I've a right to rest easy in my own bed without being dragged off to the Union to be left with a lot of flighty nurses and doctors who don't know me, and won't treat me right. Francis, I won't go, d'you hear me? I want to stay here, in my home, and if I have to suffer, I suppose I must.' She winced elaborately as she tried to move her uninjured leg, then gave a yelp of real pain.

'That hurt, did it?' Dr Pickbone began, in a calm and detached manner, to pack his things. 'Well, I dare say it might—and you know, of course, that things will only get worse. But, if you're sure that you're not going to the hospital like a sensible old lady, I don't see how I can force you.' He winked in Alice's direction. 'Perhaps, Mrs Shortcake, just before you show me out, you'd be good enough to fetch me a glass of water? I'll leave you some painkillers, Kate, since there's nothing more you need me to do—when the pain gets really severe, you'll just have to keep knocking them back—every hour or so, I expect.'

A brief flicker of pity crossed his face as her frightened eyes followed Alice, whisking herself briskly from the room; then he hardened his expression. 'I don't believe you'll be in *very* bad pain for more than, oh, a couple of months—then maybe, as the bone starts to knit on its own, things might improve . . . You'll be left with a limp, but you won't mind that, will you?'

The pills he had shaken out of a bottle were large, and round; he held them out to her. 'Take these two for now, and I'll write a repeat prescription for whenever Alice cares to ring the surgery—I won't bother coming to see you again, under the circumstances . . .'

'And where *is* Alice with my water?' gasped Kate, her eyes wide with alarm at the size of the pills. ' A poor, sick widow like me needs all the friends she's got at times like this—and a fine friend you've turned out to be to me, Francis Pickbone!'

'What, because I refuse to set your broken leg on your kitchen table? How can you ask me to do something I'm sure would be bad for you? You're being very foolish, as well you know—the proper place for you is hospital. You won't manage a proper recovery if you insist on staying here.'

There was a pause, during which he dusted invisible specks from his sleeve, and Alice, frantically eavesdropping outside, could barely contain herself. Kate soon gave a pathetic sniff: Pickbone ignored it. She sniffed again—then gave a plaintive little cough.

'Francis . . .' she said at last. He strolled across to smile down at the small plump figure with that scared, yet brave, expression. How hard she always tried to have her own way, and how he had to admire her spirit! Few people ever got the better of Kate Keepdown.

'I could ask for a second opinion,' she suggested. 'It might not be as bad as you say—I don't want to go to the Union, I don't indeed, Francis!'

'Now, Kate, do you honestly believe I'd let them do anything to harm you? Think of my Hippocratic oath! And —I tell you what—you shall have a private room, and, just as soon as you're well enough, I'll arrange for you to have a special nurse here, so you needn't stay away from home any longer than necessary. It might only be for a few days —so, how about it, Kate?'

The pause this time was longer. Once more he gathered his things together and was about to take his leave, when:

'All right—I'll go, if I must!' she cried. 'But mind, not for one moment longer than I need. Promise?'

'You have my word,' he assured her; and they both heaved deep sighs of relief, which set them laughing together. Alice now judged that it was safe to come back.

'I'll just be showing Doctor out,' she volunteered, with a sideways glance at the triumphant Pickbone. 'And where's he put them pills you're supposed to take?'

'Don't think I don't know what you've been up to, plotting and listening at doors,' came the tart reply. 'You can stop your pretending! I'm taking no pills—I'm going into hospital. I've had shouting and bullying at me so I'm not sure if I'm on my head or my heels—now, you tell 'em in the hall that they'd best be coming to fetch me, before I change my mind! Go on—be off with you!'

And Alice hurried happily away, to inform the ambulance men, with smug satisfaction, that they could collect their patient at once; and reflecting, as they obeyed her summons, that it was a rare event indeed when anyone managed to out-manoeuvre the despotic chatelaine of Swan House.

Mr William Visor of Wincot, solicitor in a firm which had handled the Keepdown affairs for several generations, sat drinking with Dr Pickbone in a quiet and pleasant pub.

'How I wish that we had been able to prevail upon Mrs Keepdown to let us advise her relatives of today's operation. At her advanced age, anything might happen—and it would look badly for us, would you not agree, if the first anyone directly connected with her affairs learned about her state of health had to come from her executors.' And, at that final word, Mr Visor coughed disapprovingly.

Pickbone grinned. 'I can't see Kate going to the hereafter for a few years yet—she's determined to live for as long as she can, just to annoy her family. And really, it isn't so much of a risk as it might have been for somebody as old as she is, say, twenty years ago—modern anaesthetics don't knock you about anything like they used to, and she'll be carefully monitored right the way through.'

'I still consider that her nieces, at least, should have been informed,' insisted Visor, but Pickbone disagreed.

'What! Kate let Marian Hacket know she's not in the very best of health? The old girl can't stand not being fully in command of herself, and everyone else—she'd hate people to see her stuck immobile in bed. Besides, she can't bear Marian—though she has the odd kind word for Cicely . . .'

'Ah, that cataract business,' nodded Visor, with a faint smile. Pickbone cursed.

'I've never been so embarrassed in my life! There stood Kate, right outside the eye-specialist's door, in the very middle of the town, screaming to high heaven that Marian and Cicely were trying to murder her! Cicely began to cry, and her sister boxed her ears—for a moment, I hoped she'd deal with Kate's hysterics the same way, but not even Marian Hacket is *that* brave. She just dragged the pair of them back to the car, and swore she'd never volunteer to help her aunt in any way ever again—and I don't believe she has. When I eventually talked the old devil into making a fresh appointment to see Sir Nicholas Gawsey, there was no mention of any of the family accompanying her—*I* went with her!'

'You displayed great courage and resource,' praised Mr Visor. 'And did you ever establish the original cause of her, um, outburst?'

'Certainly not by talking to Kate,' chuckled Pickbone, 'although, when I ran across Cicely accidentally-on-purpose later (she'd no idea that I'd witnessed the whole disgraceful scene), I gathered it was something to do with Marian's remark, just as they were walking from the car to the surgery —about Kate's needing to set her affairs well in order, just in case, before she had the operation. I suppose . . . ?'

'She has not,' replied Visor to the unvoiced question, 'and I can say nothing to persuade her otherwise. I simply do not understand why comparatively healthy old ladies are so adamant about the very discussion of the idea of making a Will! They usually end up by fretting themselves into poorer health just through their refusal to face up to their responsibilities—which is particularly distressing in the case of Mrs Keepdown, since the problem really began many years ago, when Lucian Keepdown died so suddenly, intestate—very careless indeed. At least, then, there was a clear heir in the person of his wife, but now . . .'

'It's a most oddly-set-up family,' agreed Pickbone, as his friend sighed deeply, and shook a despairing head. 'If I've understood things right, Luke's side won't get a penny when Kate eventually goes—is that true?' Visor sighed again, and nodded glumly. 'Then, surely, as her blood relations, Marian and Cicely scoop the lot?' Another sorrowful nod. 'Seems highly unfair to me,' opined the doctor; then his eyes gleamed. 'Why not try explaining to Kate—it won't be long before she's out of hospital, I'd guess—that dear Marian stands to inherit half of everything she owns, if the old girl doesn't leave a Will? She'd make fifty of 'em rather than let that happen, I'll bet what you like!'

Visor considered this. 'It seems unprofessional to suggest that it would be in my client's interests to make a Will merely for the sake of cutting someone out of it, but—my word! It is precisely the argument which might make Mrs

Keepdown see sense at last. These intestacies usually drag
on and on . . . When do you imagine I may visit her?' His
mind was made up.

'Best let her leave hospital first—I promised her that, if
I found a suitable nurse, she could come home in ten days
or so—but Kate wants to vet the girl first. I'll have to take
a few along to pass inspection—she's a bit of a snob, isn't
she? Doesn't want anyone jumped-up or not quite-quite
wandering about the house looking after her—I can see
myself horrifying the most superior nursing agencies by
asking to see bloodlines and pedigrees instead of diplomas!'

The solicitor was silent, gazing into the depths of his
schooner with no sign that he would go his round; Pickbone
drained his own glass, and set it on the table with a clunk.
Mr Visor roused himself at this reminder.

'Another sherry, I think—and for you? Of course . . .
Pickbone, I may be able to help you over this matter of a
nurse. A girl I know—friend of mine, of my wife's, that is
—nice manner, known her all my life, quiet and good at her
work—class medal and so on . . . been companioning an
ancient cousin of mine, who has now gone into a nursing-
home for good, so Jane (that is her name, Jane Nightwork)
is at a loose end—has done agency work for a time, but I
happen to know she is looking for something rather more
permanent—I could, er, give her a character reference and
so on, if you cared to consider her for the post.'

Pickbone appreciated his friend's diffidence in rec-
ommending this young person: Visor had been but recently
widowed of an alcoholic wife, and for years before this happy
release was known to make occasional trips to the peaceful
world outside his own private hell. No doubt the solicitor
questioned the ethics of suggesting the installation of his
current mistress as the medical attendant of one of his oldest
and most influential clients; but at least there could be no
harm in looking the young woman over. If she seemed as
unlikely as Visor himself to indulge in glaring breaches of
propriety (and Dr Pickbone too was no stranger to the less

wholesome aspects of professional life), it might save much trouble if this nursing *friend of the solicitor's wife* could be approved for the care of Kate Keepdown.

And she was: with the minimum of effort. The passage of two weeks saw the lady of the manor back at home, rather paler, perhaps more thoughtful, but attended by a nurse with a will as formidable as her own. Like most bullies, Kate tended to respect those who could stand up to her: Jane Nightwork stood firm upon her conviction that she was, undoubtedly, a good nurse. Tactful, unassuming, and gently skilled, she would brook no dissent, and could justify her every action with wise and reasoned argument.

Kate, not the easiest of charges, demanded more than her fair share of attention from everyone, not just Jane; but it was the nurse who most easily coped with the frequent changes of appetite, the alterations of pillows and bed-clothes, the requests for windows to be open or closed, the curtains drawn or shut. Indeed, Alice Shortcake was heard grumbling about the unexpected partiality shown by her mistress, and the newcomer's growing influence; but Dr Pickbone was pleased with his choice, and with the progress of his patient—even the two visits paid by William Visor, conducted with decorum on the part of both lover and paramour, left Kate Keepdown no worse for the experience —though it wasn't honestly possible to make the same happy claim for a frustrated Mr Visor.

'Will you please just *listen* to me, Mrs Keepdown,' the weary solicitor sighed. 'Surely you can see that it must be common sense for someone as prosperous as yourself to be absolutely insistent upon making a Will—to ensure that any particular bequests should be fully explained, and that if there might be anyone to whom you definitely did *not* wish to leave anything—'

'You want me to start cutting people out of my Will, do you? Rather than putting 'em in it? A fine idea, I must say!' But the sparkle in Kate's dark eyes belied her words, as she

tried not to chuckle at the notion of disinheriting someone
—or everyone.

He pressed home his slight advantage. 'Moreover, there
is the tenable view that it might not be exactly fair for all
the money, made by Keepdowns, to leave the family and
pass elsewhere—to those only connected by marriage. You
see, if your husband had only left everything in trust for
your lifetime, and thence to his own heirs, it would have
had precisely the same effect upon you, but would have
been less unjust to his relations—who are, after all, Keepdown heirs by birth, by ties of blood.'

'And I'm not, d'you mean?' flashed Kate. 'I'm not quite
as good as they are, hey? Well, if they've got a legal claim
to the name, let them sue the others for it after I'm gone, if
they want! I'll have nothing to do with it—and if you think
I'm going to let that black sheep Gilbert Peck have one
penny of my money, you're wrong! Not if he goes down on
his bended knees to me, he won't!'

Visor said nothing: she was adamant now, as so many of
his elderly female clients could be, but they usually came to
their senses in the end. Of course, not being a medical man,
he could not guess whether Kate Keepdown's untimely
death might cause discord in the two branches of her family
sooner than anticipated . . .

The problem had arisen way back in the previous generation, when both sets of parents (Lucian Keepdown's and
his future mate's) had produced between them few offspring
to survive to years of discretion. Kate had been spared but
one younger brother, who married twice at a twenty-five
year interval: thus acquiring a split-level family, the half-
sisters Marian and Cicely Hacket, Kate's nieces and, unfortunately, her only blood relations.

Things were no better on the Keepdown side: Lucian's
younger sister had wed, given birth, and died within the
space of one year, and her sorrowing spouse had taken
little interest in Gilbert Peck, his only child, spoiled by
nursemaids and unchastised by a weakly, barren step-

mother. The only other Keepdown heir was Henry Pimpernell, sole descendant of the elder Keepdown brother (deceased) through his only daughter, also deceased. An involved history of family hostilities meant that Henry hadn't been brought up at Swan House, but he paid duty visits there rather more than any of the others; and Kate was believed to view him with something like approval.

'Henry is your grand-nephew-by-marriage, Mrs Keepdown, and thus not your legal next of kin,' Visor tried to explain. 'If your late husband's family, in the person of Mr Peck, were to contest matters after your—that is, if any form of legal action is ever undertaken, there could be no guarantee that Mr Pimpernell would benefit in the end. And—do you consider that to be just?'

'Never you mind about that! I don't need youngsters like you telling me what I ought to be doing, or thinking, or saying—why, I remember you when your mother used to push you around in your pram! And there's plenty of time for all your nonsense later on—'

'Really, Mrs Keepdown! You cannot call professional concern over your affairs *nonsense*! I am merely trying to do my best for you, and for your heirs . . .'

At that awful word, with its intimations of mortality, Kate closed her eyes and sank back upon her pillows with a hollow groan. 'I can't listen to you any longer,' she faltered in as pale a voice as she could achieve. 'Call the nurse—call Jane. Jane!'

Miss Nightwork entered quietly, and closed the heavy oak door without slamming it, though the window was open. Mrs Keepdown twinkled her approval, then remembered that she was in a parlous state.

'Mr Visor's just going,' she whispered, 'and he's not going to upset me any more today, worrying my poor old head about business—so you can see him out, and then come back and look after me.' Her forehead creased in artistic furrows, and her nervous fingers pleated the sheet with pathetic anxiety.

'Of course I will go—I am sorry to have tired you,' Visor responded promptly. 'But, please, think over what I have said—it is not a lot to ask, is it? Just—think it over.' He assembled his papers, was grudgingly permitted to shake hands, and made his way out. Nurse Nightwork accompanied him to the door, and they made brief conversation in low tones; Visor said something which set Jane spluttering with soft laughter, and her pale blue eyes were still dancing as she obeyed Kate's peremptory summons.

'Gossiping about me behind my back, hey?' she snorted, frailty now forgotten. 'You can't fool me! But you're not here to flirt with the visitors, you're here to look after me, so you'd best get a move on with it.' She watched with a smile of triumph as the nurse fussed about, tidying the bed, straightening the sheets, feeling her patient's steady pulse, and selecting a tonic.

'Two spoons of this,' decreed Jane, 'and a cup of tea to follow to take the taste away. I had a feeling you'd need something of the sort, so I've boiled the kettle . . .'

Eyes dark as currants met steady stern blue, and Kate's were almost the first to waver. She grimaced as Jane held out the spoon, and managed to spill a good dollop or two on the saucer the nurse had prophetically placed underneath; yet when Jane brought tea, in the enormous polka-dot cup the old lady preferred, it stayed rock-like in Kate's grasp as she sipped thirstily, all pretence now gone.

'It's none of my business, I know,' ventured the nurse, 'but I hope you won't allow any distress at what Mr Visor may have said to you to cloud your judgement: he's been a good, reliable friend to me and my family for as long as I can remember, and I'm sure whatever advice he gave you was sound. Won't you think about it some more?'

'Been on at you to get round me, has he?' Surprisingly, the old lady laughed. 'Doesn't he want you to lose your patient and your job? I suppose he thinks I'll worry myself into a decline over all this Will nonsense—*he's* the one who's been doing all the worrying, let me tell you!'

'It is always sensible to make a Will,' ignoring Kate's accusation with dignity, 'but especially so if your family is large, or scattered, or—or unusual in any way—as I can't help but gather, from hearing Mrs Shortcake and the others chatting, your family is. And Mr Visor—'

'Oh, *him*! He seems to think I ought to leave my money just the way he wants, but why should I? They say blood's thicker than water, don't they? And it's mine, anyway, all of it—to leave how I want. Maybe the Cats' Home will get the lot!' Her villainous chuckle was so hearty that sudden tears began to tumble from her deep-set eyes, and she spluttered. Jane quickly fetched a handkerchief, and a glass of water.

'You're a good girl to me,' gasped the humorist at last. 'Mind you, that's what you're paid for—but, who knows? I might decide to leave the money to *you*, you know. It would be perfectly legal, wouldn't it? It's *my* money, hey!' She raised the glass in a silent, smirking toast.

Jane shook a gently reproving head. 'You mustn't make jokes like that, Mrs Keepdown. People might misunderstand.'

'They've got no business to be listening, have they! What I say to you is my affair, and nothing to do with anyone else. If I want to do something, why—I do it . . . and there will be a big surprise for 'em all, after I'm gone!'

'I think perhaps it's time you had a little nap,' said the nurse, after shrewd scrutiny of Kate's flushed face and faster breathing. 'Mr Visor's visit has over-excited you, I'm afraid —nothing serious, but if you'll just take this, it should help you to calm down . . .'

Kate was inclined to argue, but Nurse Nightwork insisted, coaxing her to swallow the pill, and sitting beside her till she started to nod. Then she slipped quietly from the room.

Old ladies having nightmares can make a lot of noise, and Kate was no exception. She half-woke from her slumbers to be confronted by shadowy horrors, conjured from the depths of her mind by all the talk of death and dissolution

—by the thought of her money-hungry relations waiting, vulture-like, for her to die, so that they could pick the rich bones of her corpse. She was hysterical by the time Jane reached her, and took a long while to be soothed: when even in her sleep she was tormented by visions, muttering and moaning to herself, talking to invisible people whose unheard responses made her whimper with distress.

Jane sat up with her patient all night, and wouldn't let Alice telephone for the doctor. Her air of knowledgeable calm infuriated the jealous housekeeper, who darkly inveighed against folk so proud they'd let others fall sick with worry rather than ask for better help; Mrs Shortcake provided her own help, by chanting in the kitchen the various healing-spells her mother and grand-dam had bequeathed her (for it was rumoured that they were witches). It was a frustration of all her gloomy expectations when, next morning, Jane reported Kate as being much improved —asking, indeed, to see Mr Visor as soon as possible.

'I hoped you would change your mind about the matter we discussed yesterday,' he began. 'I have brought all those papers we might require—that is, if I have guessed correctly the reason for your calling me in?'

'There's no point in guessing anything. I'll tell you if I want papers, and I'll tell you if I don't. Let's start by just making a few things absolutely clear! If I don't make a Will, everything I have goes to those two girls—isn't that what you've told me?'

'To your nieces, the half-sisters Marian and Cicely, yes.'

'So then that black sheep, and young Henry—they won't get a penny?'

'Should you die intestate, that is indeed the case—and, I must emphasize, that the Keepdown moneys should go beyond the family to mere chance connections is surely—'

'Chance connections nothing! They're my own flesh and blood, I'll have you know, though they're years younger than me, of course. What do I really know about 'em? About any of them? Gilbert's a nasty bit of work, and Henry's

oh-so-prim and proper, while Cicely couldn't say Boo to a
goose, and as for bossyboots Marian . . . Well, they're all
as bad as each other. I might as well leave the lot to *you*, or
that nurse out there—or even the Cats' Home!'

A high-pitched yelp of laughter cut short his startled
protest. 'Now, see here, Visor—if you want me to make a
Will, all right, I'll do it—but on *my* terms, not yours. I
don't hold with all your legal nonsense—I'm too old to be
bothered. Here's what we'll do!' She sat up in bed, her eyes
brighter than ever, and the solicitor felt a black foreboding
that she had plotted something likely to meet with his
deepest disapproval, at the very least.

'It's my birthday soon—I'll be ninety in October! So
you're to write to all four of 'em—Gilbert, Henry and the
girls (write separately to them)—they're all to come and
stay in this house with me for the whole weekend. But—not
just with me! I want you, and Francis Pickbone, and our JP
Sir Bennet Seely—everyone's to come to dinner on the same
night, and the three of you can have a good look at all my
fine relations, to decide which is the best of the bunch. You
take a good long look at the four of them—so that you three
can choose for me!'

'You cannot be serious,' gasped Visor, once he had fully
comprehended what had just been said. 'I must have misunderstood your meaning—you *cannot* wish myself, and your
doctor, and the local magistrate, to—to *pass judgement* on
your relatives . . . surely?'

'And why not, hey? You say you want me to be fair! Now,
I hardly know any of these young people, and what I know
I don't find all that impressive, on the whole—but three of
you, all pillars of the community, good men and true, nice
and impartial—can't I trust you to help me make up my
mind? If you think you'll need longer, why—come to lunch
every day, if you want. But, by the end of the weekend, I'll
want to know which one you've chosen as the best—and
then I'll abide by your decision.'

'Decision—to do what?' faltered Visor, though he knew.

'Why, to decide how to make that Will you keep going on at me about! Because I'll make one, then—oh, yes, I will! I always said they'd be surprised, after I'm gone! So I'll leave everything to whichever one you choose—and don't you try arguing with me, William Visor, because my mind's quite made up. So you'd better get yourself busy, writing to those precious relations of mine, and make sure they'll be coming here for my birthday . . . because I can tell you, if they don't—they could regret it for the rest of their lives!'

CHAPTER 2

Reasoning and remonstrance were in vain: Kate was impishly determined to follow the solicitor's original advice to the letter. Mr Visor found himself noting details of her relatives, and drafting a cautious invitation to them to celebrate her ninetieth birthday:

Dear Miss Hacket,
 I write to you on behalf of your aunt, Mrs Keepdown, whose legal adviser I am. As you know, she has not enjoyed the best of health recently, and as a consequence is anxious that all possible arrangements concerning her future testamentary dispositions should be made while she is still sound of body and mind. It is not that we anticipate any serious change in your aunt's condition either at present, or for some time to come; but she has asked me to arrange a meeting between her good self and her likely heirs.
 You are therefore invited to celebrate her ninetieth birthday at Swan House, Bardleton, during the weekend of 29th October, when the whole matter of her business affairs is to be the subject of discussion. I sincerely hope that you will be able to attend, and remain,
Yours truly . . .

Marian polished pensive spectacles on a prim lawn handkerchief: there had been *another* solicitor's letter—for Cicely. Was Aunt Kate planning to make one of them her heir? More likely it would be her sister, with the soft nature and spineless ways—and what a waste that would be! There must be Money there—even if Aunt Kate possessed no personal wealth, the house and land, if sold, might be profitably exploited. Demolish the house, build a well-ordered development of desirable residences . . . would Cicely have any idea how to use the money so sensibly obtained? Of course not! No mathematics teacher she, with tables of stocks and shares memorized daily from the *Financial Times*, and a steadily-growing savings hoard invested at high interest rates . . . With just one lump sum, Marian Hacket could be free of scholastic drudgery for the rest of her life, free to indulge in the challenge of bulls and bears, the fun of pitting her fiscal wits in order to survive.

She studied the second sentence once more. Was Mr Visor hinting that Kate's health was not all it might be? Marian's face twisted into a wry sneer: she considered her aunt's claims to a delicate constitution to be greatly exaggerated. On one occasion, she'd taken herself off to the doctor to announce quite firmly that she was dying of cancer, when a careful examination proved her to be suffering merely from piles—which hadn't (Marian knew well) prevented the old lady from completely ignoring Dr Pickbone's advice and putting herself on an invented diet guaranteed to cause much inconvenience to those involved in the buying, preparing or serving of her meals, because there was no certainty that said diet would remain constant. The elder Miss Hacket had all the fitness of scrawny fifty (apart from the occasional crippling migraine), and had small understanding of, or sympathy for, illness—quite unlike frail, foolish Cicely.

Dear Miss Hacket,
    I write to you on behalf of your aunt . . .

Marian had disappeared to work in a whirl of briefcases and hatpins, leaving her sister to start the housework. Poor Cicely—timid, troubled for years by an incurable feminine ailment and the odd fainting spell—had never succeeded in holding down a job, responsible or otherwise, for more than a few weeks, and had long since given up the unequal struggle. She stayed on at home, and let Marian deal with the business side of their life together—after all, since Marian earned the money, it was fair that Marian should organize the house-keeping. But sometimes, in fleeting moments of timid rebellion, the thought came to Cicely that it would be wonderful to have money of her very own, not coin of the realm doled out by her sister as if it were miser-minted gold.

Just a little money of her own to spend without guilt on herself, as well as on presents—perhaps used to buy frivolous clothes, a silk nightdress, an exotic hat; a chance to travel, to stay in hotels with waiters and room-service and solid silver cutlery, clean sheets on the beds every day and hot, full baths every night, cleaned by somebody else every morning. And presents—proper, bought gifts instead of home-made sweets or hand-sewn lavender bags . . . Would her usual sort of offering please Aunt Kate, who was so very old and, Cicely thought, so very rich? Would it be politic to suggest to Marian that they withdrew some of their savings, long hoarded in the building society? Or might Marian refuse to go, despite the insistent tone of the solicitor's letter —would she ever forgive and forget the Great Cataract Row? Poor Aunt Kate, so old—so *lonely* . . . And Cicely had the sudden, sinking vision of herself in sixty-five years' time, childless and solitary, with no close family to invite to celebrate her birthday with her.

Dear Mr Peck,
    I write to you on behalf of your aunt . . .

Gilbert, the black sheep, was a florid-faced rake with a

wicked sparkle to his eyes, his conversation, and his whole
way of life. His saturnine good looks had led to a series of
problems similar to those which had caused him to be
sent down from Cambridge: shaky signatures on cheques,
long-running debts, and affiliation orders rumoured by the
dozen—which rumours only rendered him all the more
attractive to a certain type of woman.

His current amour was the screen personality Perigenia,
whose very name sent erotic shivers down the spines of ten
million men; whose slinky pin-ups cheered the walls of
countless lonely lechers admiring the honey-gold skin and
glowing emerald gaze of that sultry blonde with the sinuous,
shapely frame. She had coiled that frame close to Gilbert
one happy night when he was on a winning streak in
a gambling club; her suggestive movements and throaty
murmurs soon persuaded him to cash in his chips and take
her on to the flat—not his own, but borrowed from one of
his many acquaintances, for Gilbert Peck was an inveterate
scrounger.

Perigenia wasn't long duped by the ostentatious display
of the borrowed flat, but she stayed; for Gilbert's sexual
athleticism, despite his years (forty-five, if pressed to admit
it), suited her well. Gilbert wasn't duped by her protestations of affection, but he encouraged her to stay; he
found her as enjoyable in bed as she found him—and yet,
recently, a hint of doubt as to the wisdom of prolonging the
relationship had crept in. The lady expected him to indulge
too many of her expensive tastes with money he couldn't,
legally, hope to own: furs, jewels, and (he very much feared)
drugs, all cost money—and, with no films in the offing, she
was at a loose end as well as being impoverished—a state
she clearly thought he would subsidize.

If only she hadn't wriggled her way into his senses so
deeply that she was as much of a drug to him as he guessed
(but never dared to ask outright) heroin or cocaine must be
to her! But Gilbert was growing older, slowing down; one
day, women wouldn't fling themselves at him as they now

did—or, rather, had done: Perigenia would tolerate not a wink, not an ogle, not a rival in her life. But basically, she was too sexy for him to deny—and it could ruin him to keep on living at this pace. If only he had some money . . .

And Gilbert Peck decided, in view of the solicitor's timely letter, to ingratiate himself firmly with the aged aunt at Swan House. Even Kate's frequently-voiced dislike of her graceless nephew-by-marriage could hardly (he hoped) withstand the notorious Peck charm—but, if it could, then he would have to think of something else . . .

Dear Mr Pimpernell,
    I write to you on behalf of your aunt . . .

Henry read the letter, twice, carefully, and looked across at his friend and lodger, Matthew Goffe.

'Why on earth do you suppose my old aunt's asked her solicitor to invite me to stay for her birthday?'

'I expect she's having a party, and can't be bothered to write for herself,' suggested Matthew. 'Isn't she the one who's about a hundred years old, and filthy rich?'

'Aunt Kate will be ninety in October, and I haven't the faintest idea whether she's rich or not,' frowned Henry.

Matthew grinned. 'I've posted your letters for you sometimes, don't forget, and I've seen the address. Just the house, and the town—no street, no number. To live in a place like that, you've *got* to be filthy rich!'

Henry tutted disapprovingly at Matthew, whose communist pretensions amused, but occasionally annoyed, his landlord. Mr Goffe was a love-child whose foster parents, both dead, had never bothered to adopt him; thus having been deprived of any small share in their estate (by their legal heir), he came to see himself as a second-class citizen. Hence, his embracing of the Red cause, his support for revolution, euthanasia, and social equality; and his position as shop steward, in a factory making ladies' boned undergarments. Henry was on the clerical side, and the two met over a lost consignment of elastic-sided roll-on stays, striking up an unlikely, but rewarding, friendship.

'I haven't been to see Aunt Kate for ages—far longer than it ought to have been,' murmured Henry. 'When I was a kid I used to spend some of my holidays there—and, apart from Gilbert,' (Mr Goffe, who'd met Mr Peck and didn't view him as a kindred spirit, gave an expressive snort) 'she's just about my only living relative, I suppose. I wonder—what's the idea of all this, exactly?' He scanned the letter once more, folded it neatly into its envelope, and began to clear away the breakfast things, while Matthew ostentatiously rustled the pages of the *Morning Star*: Mr Goffe did not approve of inherited wealth.

The young men took it in turns to do the washing-up: as Henry would clean, rinse and dry methodically, so would his friend indulge in happy sloshings until he ran out of space, whereupon he would leave it all to drain. Today, as he thoughtfully squeezed bubbles in and out of a scrubber-backed sponge, Henry's forehead was wrinkled in concentration; the mention of Gilbert Peck had set him puzzling over what was being planned by their troublesome relative, wondering if the happy family celebrations might be marred by the presence of squabbling, scheming self-seekers . . .

He was too well-bred to name (even in thought) one who'd enjoyed the Pimpernell hospitality. Gilbert, whose lifestyle so displeased his staid cousin, was surprisingly willing to drop in from time to time to regale Henry (and Matthew, if he was there) with tall tales of Life Among the Smart Set—to which Henry politely listened. Afterwards, both he and Gilbert felt better for that fleeting glimpse of an alien, contrasting way of living; yet they would hardly call each other friends. A whole weekend in (presumably) Gilbert's company wasn't something to which Henry looked forward with rejoicing, particularly if Kate's ill-health (and was she really ill? It was hard to tell) cast its anticipated blight on the proceedings . . .

His mind made up, he gave the mop a final squeeze, and

went to the telephone. 'Mr Visor? Henry Pimpernell—I've just received your letter . . . Yes, of course, I knew she'd broken her leg, but I understood . . . You're sure there's nothing to worry about otherwise? . . . *All* her relations? I expected just myself, and probably Mr Peck . . . The Hackets? I remember them from a few meetings . . . Anybody else?'

Mr Visor was cautious in his reply, and in what followed: but, when Henry put down the receiver, he was far more thoughtful than before.

Of course, not everyone views with alarm, dismay or annoyance the summons from an elderly relation to pay a visit: some people welcome them. Detective-Superintendent Quentin Lees was one.

My dear Quentin,
   Well, here I am, and settled into the new house at last, apart from the smell of fresh paint in a few rooms. Thank you for the flowers, by the way—a kind thought.
   How do you like being promoted? I suppose they keep you pretty busy now, but if you could spare the time, it would be lovely to see you to catch up on all your news. *Could* you spare a few days for your great-aunt? I'd love to hear all about your new job, though I won't have anything nearly so interesting to tell you in return—all anybody in Bardleton seems to do is talk, and I already know much more about people in this village than I ever did back in the North—and I'm sure they know all about me, as well! But it's kindly meant, on the whole, and I do so enjoy a good gossip—Silence by name but not silent by nature, isn't that what I've always said?
   Why not come to stay for the weekend of October 29th? By then the smell of paint in the spare room ought to be properly gone. At the moment, it makes me sneeze every time I go in there, and I'm sure it's all been too much for poor Pooter. He hasn't really been himself since we

moved, even though generally we're settling in pretty well. I think you'll enjoy a few days here with us . . .

And Lees, writing cheerfully to accept his Aunt Ellen's invitation, looked forward to a restful weekend, a change of scene, and a good, gossipy reunion.

He certainly didn't expect murder to intrude . . .

At Swan House, preparations for Kate's great day were in full swing. From her sickbed, she hectored, organized, and fumed at her impotence; Jane Nightwork soothed, dosed, and companioned; while Alice Shortcake cook-housekeepered about the place in a permanent bustle, tramping up and down the stairs for instruction, counter-instruction and argument. In the end, Jane decided to ban Mrs Shortcake's visits as too stimulating for the invalid, in her nervous state; and passed on all future orders, suitably bowdlerized, to Kate's staff: who did not love the newcomer any more for her uninvited interference.

Jane supervised Susan Grindstone's furniture-shifting and room-freshening, Alice's linen-laundering (as required), and the sorting out of the pantry. This foetid little hidey-hole, in which Humphrey Hour was thought to drink himself into a stupor every night of the week except the Sabbath, was metamorphosed, under the nurse's watchful eye, into a clean, tidy, well-stocked cellar.

It was during this last operation that Jane, blessed by Providence with a methodical mind and a head for figures, discovered, upon glancing through such scrappy records as Hour had bothered to keep, that the butler had been slowly fiddling the books for years, as well as drinking the stock. It wasn't really her business; yet her patient's welfare was paramount, and Kate (if she learned of her servant's crime) was hardly well enough for the anticipated showdown. Though the nurse couldn't expect to dismiss him herself, she still felt that something ought to be done about it.

In her predicament, she turned to Alice, enthroned at the

white-tiled kitchen table, cracking eggs into a bowl and yelling orders to Susan in the scullery.

'Mrs Shortcake,' began Jane without preamble, 'there's a rather important matter I wish to discuss with you—but in private, if you don't mind,' as Susan gaped, and tried to hide herself behind the mangle.

'You go and hang the washing out, never mind of the rest for now, my girl,' a scandal-frustrated Susan was commanded. Miss Grindstone, befrothed to the elbows, went, angrily rattling her pegbag; Alice settled herself for a comfortable talk. At last, that nurse had recognized the cook is queen of the household . . . 'I got to watch that lazy Susan, every minute of the day,' she remarked confidentially, 'for she's as nosey as they come. You got to keep folk of her sort in their place, haven't you? Else they can do lord-knows-what, taking advantage, and presuming,' Alice nodded, and winked in a conspiratorial manner.

'Quite so,' replied Jane drily; and by her tone confirmed an enemy for life. To dare to talk so haughty to a cook in her own kitchen! 'So what was it you wanted to say to me?' snapped Mrs Shortcake, a dagger-dart in her green eyes.

'Mrs Keepdown asked me to select some drinks for all the menus, so I've had to go through the books to find out what was in stock—and—well, it seems to me that something—odd has been going on in that area for quite some time.'

'And what d'you mean by that, exactly?'

'Very odd indeed . . . I mean that the books, such as they are, have been very poorly kept, without order or method —moreover, any mistakes in the accounts always seem, funnily enough, to be in Hour's own favour.'

'Oh, do they indeed! That's what you say, is it?'

'It is, and they do. I don't want to worry or disturb Mrs Keepdown at this stage in her recovery, but I feel that such a fraud—if it is a fraud—shouldn't be permitted to continue unchecked any longer. Perhaps you could speak to Hour?'

Or should we ask Mr Visor? And, of course, you keep your own records of expenditure, so you should—'

But she was not allowed to complete her suggestion that Alice should assume responsibility for the cellar books too, using her inside knowledge to see if matters could be set right in a straightforward fashion.

'Ho!' cried Alice, boiling into temper. 'I suppose you think that just because there's maybe something out of the ordinary with the butler's books, there's something wrong with mine, too? That's slander, that is—blackening of my name, and Humphrey Hour as well—maybe it's you as don't properly understand our systems, what's bin doing of them long before you was born. And in any case, my lady, what goes on downstairs ain't none of your business, whether the missus asks you or no, for we've all bin here a sight longer nor you have, and will be when you're gone, too!'

Jane's attempted explanation was drowned out by furious culinary clamour as Alice, lips tightly primmed, viciously creamed butter and sugar in a china bowl. Routed by the din, the nurse left without another word; she breathed heavily as she went upstairs, never noticing the bright, evil eye of Hour following her until she was out of sight. He heard Kate's door tapped, opened, and closed; then he went in slippered haste to the kitchen, and his ally.

The old lady looked up from her nodding doze as the nurse entered, and immediately demanded higher pillows, hot drinks, and fresh air. Jane attended to these wants without speaking, still wondering what to do, and whether to worry anyone about the problem of Hour—perhaps Mr Visor . . .

'Penny for 'em,' challenged Kate, as Jane sighed, and sat down by the bed. 'Trying to decide if I'm really off my head, hey? So that Visor and the others won't feel they've got to pay any attention to the wishes of an old girl like me?'

'You certainly are not off your head, Mrs Keepdown,' a shocked Jane hurried to reassure her. 'Who's been saying that you might be?'

'Anyone who knows I've decided to let three people who are supposed to have plenty of common sense between 'em all choose which of my relations ought to get my money! I know that's what everyone will be saying about me!'

Jane was silent; Kate chuckled. 'Now you're wondering if I mightn't be crazy, after all, even to consider it—but it seems a very sensible idea to me, when I hardly know any of my precious relations—do I?'

'It's certainly unusual, though I can't call it crazy—but you shouldn't be talking to me about it, Mrs Keepdown. Your business affairs are nothing to do with me—I'm only your nurse, and they are your private concern.'

'And you're my private nurse, aren't you?' Kate clapped her plump hands together, feeling she'd scored a point. 'Well, if you won't let me talk about it—and you won't let me leave it to you—why, I dare say the Cats' Home will get the lot—you wait and see how surprised they'll be!'

And she burst into laughter, shrill and exhausting. Jane had to quieten her with firm words and medicine, and knew that, whether she wished the burden of Hour's misdeeds to be removed from her own shoulders or not, Kate Keepdown was not the person to do it just yet.

William Visor, she already knew, wouldn't be coming again to Swan House until the end of next week: by which time, Jane reasoned, Kate should be well enough to deal with Hour herself, after all. Or, at the least—well enough to be able to instruct Mr Visor to do so . . .

Because the interest of the patient must always come first, for a conscientious nurse.

CHAPTER 3

The next few days were rather tricky for everybody except Kate, on whose behalf there arose an unspoken conspiracy to maintain her invalid's ignorance of the undercurrents of friction at Swan House. Jane Nightwork's task of passing on instructions to staff who doggedly united in refusing to communicate with her was particularly awkward; yet she did her best, since her patient was still too excitable to be permitted to see Alice, found Susan infuriatingly stupid, and didn't want Hour to see her in her nightgown.

She wore bedroom attire less and less as time passed. Dr Pickbone, after careful examination, had produced a walking frame which Kate, conceited as ever, struggled to master in time for her first public appearance: the little supper-party she'd planned for Pickbone, Visor, and the Justice of the Peace, Sir Bennet Seely—none of whom must witness her undignified lurchings. She would hide the frame and be discovered, already sitting, as the guests arrived; and would remain seated until after they had gone.

'And you're to be with me, girl,' she informed Jane with a determined air. 'Nothing's to go wrong, so I'll need you just in case I have to move about, won't I?'

'But Dr Pickbone—' protested the nurse.

'Francis will be here to talk business, same as the rest. You're here to look after me, aren't you? Well then, do it! I dare say in your job you've learned how to stop listening when you ought, or to forget when you must—so I expect you there, miss, and no fancy dressing-up, either. If you've got your uniform on, the others will understand.'

Jane still demurred, but her employer became peevish, so the nurse consoled herself with the thought that it would, indeed, be in her patient's interests to have a medical attendant beside her at this Judges' Supper. Moreover, she was surprised to find that she too was infected by Kate's gleeful anticipation of coming events: after a tragically mis-managed love-affair, Jane had believed her emotions to have been so scarred that she was capable of nothing except calm and dispassionate feelings towards others—yet here she was, almost as eager as Kate Keepdown to see what would happen at the first, and subsequent (if any), meetings of this triumvirate tribunal of financial advisers.

Much wrangling accompanied the drawing-up of the supper-party menu, which Kate (predictably) enjoyed; Jane wondered if this constant bickering and frequent rearrangement could in any way harm her patient, when a nurse's instincts were for a settled, soothing recovery. She mentioned her fears to Dr Pickbone, who soon put her right.

'Why, the old devil positively thrives on it! She's well past the risk of post-operative shock, she's regaining mobility and strength, and she really relishes a good scrap, our Kate. Let her convalesce how she wants, within reason, and you'll soon be on your way—and wouldn't you rather have a fighter than a creaking gate as a patient?'

'She certainly doesn't seem to let anything get her down for long,' smiled Jane. 'She bounces back fast enough!'

Pickbone nodded. 'I've only ever seen Kate Keepdown *kept* down for more than a few minutes when her husband died so suddenly—she was desolate then, and I half thought she'd go into a decline from shock—his heart, you see, walking round the fields early one morning and off he went, leaving her to pick up the pieces—which she did in the end. And I've never known anything else beat her for long!'

'It's wonderful how she finds the energy, at her age.'

'She hasn't changed over the years, so it's probably just habitual cussedness,' grinned Pickbone. 'My father was the GP here before me, and said she was exactly the same as a bride. An elopement, it was—she met young Lucian Keepdown at a spa or something (he was one of those delicate younger brothers on a water-cure) and ran away with him, in spite of her chaperone and his sidekick. Six weeks later they turned up here, bold as brass—Kate may not have breeding, but you can't fault her on courage! She outfaced the lot of them, even though they never forgave him for marrying out of the County—but there was an accident, and she lost her baby and could never have another —so his father and brother disliked her even more, and then the brother died. Bardleton folk still say it was the realization

that Kate would end up lady of the manor that killed off
old Keepdown years before his time!

'Oh well, it was all a long time ago—and look at us,
gossiping like a pair of housewives! I've other calls to make
. . . So, tell Alice Shortcake to go ahead and cook anything
within reason, and things should be fine. I'm trusting you
to make sure Kate doesn't overeat, though!'

'I suppose Mrs Shortcake also remembers Mrs Keepdown
from way back?' asked Jane idly, as the doctor shrugged on
his coat. 'She has the air of an old family retainer.'

'Yes, indeed. She and her brother—they're twins, did you
know?—both started in service here when they were just
fourteen, a year or so after Kate was married. Of course,
Alice was only the scullery-maid then, and her brother was
the boot-boy, but they've all grown old together, and seen
many changes. Cook-housekeeper and butler, now . . .'

'Butler?' exclaimed Jane. 'The butler is Mrs Shortcake's
brother? Why—I had no idea.'

'Oh yes,' said Pickbone, hurrying on his way. 'She was
Alice Hour before she married the footman—he was killed
in the last war, but she'd never had any intention of leaving
this place, and neither had her brother—they'll live and die
here, and see both of us out, I shouldn't wonder.'

'I see,' murmured Jane absently. 'Oh dear, yes—I see.'

William Visor had been instructed to invite himself and the
two others on seven-for-seven-thirty terms, but resolved to
arrive early for one more attempt at private persuasion. He
also quietly warned both Sir Bennet and Pickbone of what
Kate might have planned, and went so far as to express
tentative doubts about her sanity to the doctor.

'Rubbish!' he was rebuked. 'She's as sane as you or I,
and as shrewd an old girl as you'll meet. Why not let her
amuse herself with this nonsense? I'll bet that she listens
carefully to whatever advice she lets us give, and then she
makes up her mind to do something completely different—
I know my Kate Keepdown,' laughed Pickbone. 'For my

part, I intend to have a pleasant meal among good company, and to the devil with the rest of the charade. Forget it, man!'

'Is that your medical diagnosis?' inquired the solicitor, with the beginnings of a smile. 'I suppose you could well be right—but I shudder to think of the headlines in the popular press, or what the Law Society might say—'

'Oh, lawyers be damned! I'd be happy to go into a court of law this very minute and swear that your client was in her entirely right mind when she put forward the original proposal, when she invited us three round to ask for our opinions—*and* when she later on took absolutely no notice of them! You know, you worry far too much.'

'Maybe I do,' sighed Visor, 'but . . . You and I must try to get there before Sir Bennet on Friday, if possible. I would like to have one more talk with Mrs Keepdown before being forced to undergo this unprofessional folly—and, as her legal adviser, I would appreciate some word from you as her *medical* adviser that she was mentally sound . . .'

Pickbone tried not to laugh at the solicitor's pleading expression. 'Oh, the legal mind! How it revels in hedging bets and providing for all eventualities! Oh, very well—I'll come along and certify that she's healthy, and sane, if it'll make you any happier—say, just before seven?'

But Fate interfered with this comfortable arrangement in the form of a commuting client who'd come home to find that his wife had run off with the milkman. By the time Visor had queried the wisdom of changing the locks, booby-trapping the front gate, and contesting custody of the poodle, he was late. Then he went out to the garage—to discover a puncture in his front tyre, which would make him even later. Under his car and under his breath, he cursed, hoping that Pickbone, at least, had been able to play his part.

The doctor was announced by a flustered Susan, for Hour had fortified himself too strongly against the rigours of so rare an occurrence as guests. Pickbone walked over to the firm, high-backed chair where Kate sat in splendour, and, shaking her hand, asked politely how she was.

This courtesy set her cackling. 'Francis, you'll be the death of me yet! You were here only this morning, weren't you? Shall I stick out my tongue again and say *ninety-nine?* Or do you want to tap my kneecaps with your little hammer? You know perfectly well how I am!'

Pickbone grinned. Jane hid a smile: it wasn't for a nurse to criticize a doctor, no matter how amusing the opportunity. Kate chuckled again at her dilemma, and poked the doctor with her swagger-stick.

'Never mind, Francis, you've got a lovely bedside manner *and* a lovely visiting manner. Now, go and pour yourself a drink—and me too—and what about you, girl? Are nurses allowed to drink on duty, or am I muddling you with policemen? Thank goodness I don't need a gaoler yet—or a keeper, either,' she added sharply, as Pickbone glanced at her. The last laugh had left her rather breathless, and she was wheezing; but he saw nothing to alarm him greatly.

'You will have your little joke, Kate,' he smiled, moving over to the newly-polished silver tray. 'But you may also have your little drink—both of you. What would you—oh.'

The selection wasn't wide, for Hour had been inoperative since early that afternoon, and Susan had thought to provide only ice, without checking the contents of the tray. Pickbone puzzled over the curious choice before crying:

'I'll mix you one of my famous Specials—my Guaranteed Cure-All Concoction! Is there a tall jug I could use?'

As Kate gave instructions to Jane, the door opened, and Susan announced Sir Bennet Seely. Empire builders are commonly thought to be brick-red persons, moustached, monocled and megaphone-voiced: Seely was small and faded, shrivelled in an ill-fitting suit, his moustache a wispy memory, his tenor pipe querulous and bland. Though for his late spinster sister's sake there was no great liking between Kate and the little baronet, he maintained a polite intercourse with the manor; and now advanced to shake his hostess's hand, and to find himself pressed into service.

'Seely, just in time! You must assist at the operation, if

you'd be so kind—I'm about to do myself and my colleagues
out of a job by preparing a generous helping of Pickbone's
Guaranteed Cure-All Concoction, for the relief of athlete's
foot, housemaid's knee, and dhobi's itch . . .' The doctor
took bottles, opened them, sniffed each in turn; poured,
stirred ('Scalpel—I mean spoon, please, Seely,') and tasted.
It was the perfect pastiche of a medical demonstration.
Kate chuckled throughout; Jane Nightwork, whose training
allowed her to appreciate the finer points of the performance,
was silent, in thought. Possibly the slightly questionable
taste of the doctor's joke in the house of an elderly invalid
was troubling her.

However, it didn't seem to trouble her patient; Kate
accepted her own glass of Cure-All with a twinkle, then
prodded Jane sharply with the swagger-stick. 'Wake up,
girl, do, and enjoy my party! Cheers to you all!'

'Long life and good health to you, Kate,' responded
Pickbone. Sir Bennet grudgingly raised his glass; Jane, with
an apologetic smile for her slowness, followed suit. But her
distrait air was overlooked in the tardy arrival of the final
guest, half an hour late and smelling of oil.

His own apologies accomplished, Mr Visor took his glass
of Pickbone's fearsome cocktail, to pronounce it excellent:
'One glass is all I would risk, if I had to drive my car
afterwards!' Evidently Seely didn't think the same way, for
he drained his glass and required the doctor, for politeness'
sake, to pour him a second. Nobody else followed his brave
example, however, and, as the ice clinked in the empty jug,
Susan announced supper.

The meal was wheeled in on a creaking trolley, massive
pewter covers keeping the dishes warm. The three men
made conversation together as Jane helped Kate the short
distance to her seat, and placed herself to the left of her
hostess; Seely was directed to Kate's right, with the solicitor
and the doctor settled below the salt.

William Visor assisted Jane to seat herself before pulling
out his own chair, one of a handsome Georgian set, like the

table mahogany, with carved hooks on the sides for the attachment of wicker firescreens. In order to show off her treasures, Kate had ordered a fire to be lit, and as flames flickered and sparks flew up the chimney, the air gradually warmed, tinged with a gentle burning scent.

Susan ladled soup, spilling only two drops on the fine damask cloth; Kate scolded, and threatened to box her ears if she repeated the offence, and Susan sniffed. Jane gave her patient an appraising look as she wheezed: was it all the pepper, or was it too much excitement?

Dr Pickbone laughed at her. 'I've already told you that Mrs Keepdown can have a little of whatever she likes, within reason—you nurses are all the same. Fuss, fuss, fuss!'

Visor deftly turned the conversation. 'Let me see, Miss Nightwork—how long is it that you have been nursing here? About three weeks, I believe?'

She nodded gratefully. 'Just over two and a half.'

'And would you not say, Pickbone, that my recommendation was a success? Mrs Keepdown looks in excellent health.'

'And so I should, with what I'm paying for the privilege!' Kate assured him, while the doctor smothered a grin at the decorous distance the lovers imposed between themselves in public. He found his patient's quick black bright eye upon him, and hastened to agree with Mr Visor.

'Miss Nightwork has been invaluable. There are few folk brave enough to try to tell you what to do, Kate, and how to look after yourself, but I think we've got one here!'

'Tell me what to do? I'd like to see anyone try!' snorted the old lady, delighted. 'You'd better not do anything of the sort, Francis Pickbone—why, I remember—'

'—me when my mother used to push me about in my pram,' he concluded briskly; and they all chuckled. Slowly, the party began to relax, the guests to enjoy themselves; Kate drank wine with gusto, and urged the others to do so too.

'I'll have no heeltaps,' she told them severely. 'Let's open another bottle—what d'you all say, hey?'

William Visor and Jane looked up from their plates simultaneously, nodding a smiling acceptance; Kate watched the firelight dance its shadows around the room and across their faces, and scowled at Sir Bennet, who'd drained his glass almost before she finished speaking, and now sat waiting, with an eager look in his eye.

Susan scuttled about, doing her best, and not doing too badly, either. Dr Pickbone, causing much laughter by his remarks, removed the cork from the second bottle—a task Kate couldn't trust to Susan's clumsiness. Then Miss Grindstone was chided again for the niggardly helpings of fresh fruit or plum pudding with which she would serve her mistress, for Kate wanted both, and heaped goodies on her plate with a liberal hand, adding greedy dollops of cream in a decided manner which had Jane looking anxiously at Dr Pickbone, while he shrugged his shoulders in resignation.

Coffee was brought, and Kate refused the gentlemen brandy, insisting that all must drink port, which she preferred; and, once the bottle had made its circuit of the table and come to rest temporarily in the middle:

'Now then,' said Kate Keepdown, 'to business!'

Jane Nightwork and William Visor both began to speak at once; looked quickly at each other; smiled, spoke again; and burst out laughing. Pickbone regarded them with an indulgent air, but hoped that Kate, so strict and unforgiving, hadn't guessed their true relationship: he knew how she'd feel about it! Perhaps more strongly than many of her generation; but it was, after all, her house, and they were both in her employ. Should he rush into the conversation to divert it, as Mr Visor had done earlier?

Kate forestalled him. 'Ladies first, ladies first, that was how I was brought up,' she frowned. Nevertheless it was Visor who replied, as Jane hesitated.

'I believe I can guess what Miss Nightwork has to say— we have enjoyed a most pleasant meal together, but—'

'But nothing! Ladies first, remember? Speak up, girl!'

Jane glanced from the solicitor to her patient, and gave

a perplexed flick of her eyebrows before taking a very deep breath. 'Mrs Keepdown, I simply can't feel it right for me to attend any private family discussions you may wish to have, and I'm sure Mr Visor agrees with me—even though he knows that you can always rely upon my discretion. But I would much prefer not to be present!' At once, she made to leave her seat; Visor, with a nod of approval, hurried to assist her, pulling back her chair and addressing Kate over the nurse's bowed blonde head.

'Miss Nightwork is entirely correct in her attitude, I assure you, Mrs Keepdown, and, as your legal adviser, I do insist that if you are determined to enter upon this course of action—against which I have counselled you before, and was about to do so again—well, she should not remain. If your state of health gives rise to any alarm—'

'There's nothing wrong with me!' flashed Kate, glaring at the conspirators standing side by side, defiant in the firelight. She gave one of her sudden wicked cackles. 'Be off with you then, girl, only mind—if I die of a heart attack, William Visor, it'll be all your fault for encouraging this child to neglect her duties!'

'You won't die for years yet, Kate,' Pickbone told her, grinning. 'Never less likely in your life, if you'd care for my professional opinion—you'll outlive us all just to annoy eveyone, if I know you.'

'Ha!' cried Kate, pleased yet thwarted, as Jane silently withdrew. Sir Bennet rushed into the breach with timely courtesy, by requesting permission to smoke.

Mrs Keepdown graciously consenting, he produced a slim silver cigarette case, which he offered in turn to Pickbone and Visor. The whole room reeled about them, however, when Kate inquired testily:

'And what about me, then, hey, Seely?'

'Kate, how long has this been going on?' demanded the doctor, with a grin across the table at the baronet.

'Never you mind,' she retorted, taking a cigarette with a triumphant smirk. Sir Bennet drew out his lighter, and offered the tiny flame to the wavering tip; Kate inhaled, and never even blinked. The end of the cigarette glowed—she blew defiant smoke rings towards Pickbone, one after the other; the men applauded her skill, and she preened herself for a moment. Then, all at once, she pounced.

'Now then—to business, everyone!' said Kate Keepdown.

The four voices rose and fell, Kate's most insistent of all, as Jane sat in a deep armchair, waiting for the summons to help her recalcitrant charge to bed. The words were mostly indistinct, but the general sense was clear: nothing, and nobody, could dissuade Kate Keepdown from her idea of a jury to select her eventual heir.

Jane had to smile; and she hoped she might be even half as indomitable when her ninetieth birthday approached. But then she sighed, recalling that she'd probably be (unless the ice about her heart should melt, and she should marry) as lonely as this old lady, or worse. Kate had four possible heirs, Jane knew: but she could think of no one close to herself by blood or affection—not now.

Perhaps Kate had already made up her mind, and was playing a deep game for the sheer mischief of it; probably the quiet one of those two nieces (Celia? Cynthia?) would be the one to inherit eventually, or that Henry (What?) of whom the servants, before their quarrel with the nurse, had spoken with some affection. Though Jane always tried to avoid listening to gossip, she couldn't help knowing that at Swan House both staff and mistress had a proud sense of family position and responsibility, of tradition—in Mrs Keepdown, more than might be expected, in a way, since she had, after all, only married into the manor, not been born there . . .

'She's ready to go up now, Nurse,' Dr Pickbone roused her from her reverie, surprised she had elected to sit in the uncertain light from an open fire without even candles to cheer the room, as there had been at dinner. 'Better give her a sedative tonight,' he added quietly, closing the sitting-room door behind him. 'She's enjoyed all the arguing, of course, but we don't want her over-excited and unable to sleep—have you enough tablets, or shall I look in my car?'

'There's no need to bother, thank you, Doctor. I've not used as many as you originally thought, so I have an ample supply for the next few days, I believe.'

'Nevertheless, I'll send over a further lot tomorrow—I think you'll begin to need them now, with all the bother of next weekend ahead of her—but I hope you'll take good care of them. I'll prescribe a double dose tonight, which should settle her nicely—only we don't want any mistakes. At her age, it could be dangerous.'

'You can trust me to take the utmost care in my dealings with my patient, Doctor,' replied Jane stiffly. He flushed, muttered something, and escorted her in silence to the dining-room.

Grumbling under her breath, Kate was eased from her chair so that she might stand to bid her guests farewell. First to thank her for an interesting evening was a thoughtful Sir Bennet; Mr Visor was about to follow him when Kate, her dark eyes snapping, said imperiously:

'Just a moment! I want to talk to you—in private.' A piercing look was directed at Jane and the doctor, who were hovering professionally nearby. 'I can manage on my own for a few minutes, you know—so you can both go away. Go on, be off with the pair of you—wait outside!'

'No more than two minutes, Kate, d'you hear me?' Pickbone scolded as, perforce, he left the room with Jane.

'Stuff and nonsense,' retorted the old lady, grinding the metal tip of her swagger-stick into the carpet. Left alone with her, Visor gave a perplexed flick of his eyebrows before venturing to ask: 'May I assume that you have, even now, thought better of this scheme, Mrs Keepdown?'

'Ha!' cried Kate. 'Never you mind *my* affairs—I want to talk about yours! That girl—is she your daughter?'

He scuffled his feet in dumb embarrassment, and paled.

'Come on, man, speak up—yes or no? But of course she

is, I could see the resemblance this evening all right. I can't think why I didn't before . . . Does she know?'

He found his voice. 'She does not. She knows me only as an old friend of her mother. I could never marry as I would have wished, with my poor wife the way she was—and, by the time she died last year, it was too late, Jane's mother was already dead. Jane does not know, and I do not intend that she shall—I see no reason for burdening her with my, with our relationship. She is making her way in the world, and believes herself to be a posthumous child—which is how it must remain, for both our sakes.'

'Francis Pickbone,' exulted Kate, 'doesn't know—thinks she's your mistress! I could tell from the way he was looking at you both tonight. Well, he's a fool—and a tolerant, lax fool at that, if he's prepared to let a girl of sinful birth take care of me. And you! How can you talk of professional responsibilities, when you litter the countryside with your bastards? Introducing them to this house, worming their way into the place—and she *seems* such a nice child, too. I wonder what she'd say if she knew the truth?'

'You must not tell her!' His voice trembled: whether from rage or shame, it was hard to say. 'I forbid you to mention this to her—I beg you, in common humanity!'

'*Common* is right,' returned Kate, 'though I suppose your morals, low as they are, can have nothing to do with me— except where they involve my own concerns. If I had enough time to arrange it, I'd look for someone else for next weekend —I can't feel able to trust you any more. But, *after* then, I'll be taking my legal business elsewhere—it must be the last job I can permit you to do for me. Don't argue! I never heard of such goings-on—there's to be nothing of *that* sort in *my* house! Your bastard, hey!'

'Please do not tell her,' begged an anguished Mr Visor. 'The fault was mine, mine and her mother's—we knew, all the time, that we could never honourably marry—but must our child have to bear the sadness and shame of it all? Think of her—of the shock—'

'Shock? *Shock?* What about me? You brought her here under false pretences—you lied to me—you, a solicitor!'

He drew himself up, breathing hard. 'I recommended to your physician a private nurse of high professional competence, and I cannot consider such action to have been a breach of trust. Pickbone was satisfied with his choice— after careful inquiry, I remind you—and, until now, you have expressed the same satisfaction. I ask you again to think of what you threaten—think of the scandal!'

'Are you worried for her sake or yours?' flared Kate.

'My only concern must be for the health and happiness of—of my daughter. It is my wish that she should live a safe and untroubled life—these things may not be frowned upon as much as they used to be—'

'Except by *me*,' pronounced Kate awfully.

'—but I still would not wish her to have the shadow of illegitimacy over her career and opportunities.' With grim determination, he went on, 'You are at liberty to remove your affairs from my firm, of course, but I would point out that we have given good service for three generations now, and would like to continue so to do. However, if you intend to—to act against my wishes in this matter of my daughter, I shall find every possible means to prevent you. If Pickbone has to remove Jane from here and leave you without a medical attendant, I would gladly urge it, to protect her. But—please do not force me to do this.'

'Are you trying to frighten me, William Visor?'

'No more than you are trying to intimidate me, Mrs Keepdown. Please listen to me—leave things as they are. I beg you—say nothing about this to my daughter.'

'Your *illegitimate* daughter—ha! We'll have to see about that—who knows what might happen?'

'Who knows indeed, Mrs Keepdown?' said Mr Visor softly. 'Who knows?'

CHAPTER 4

William Visor's abrupt departure from Swan House meant that Jane had no chance to speak to him about Hour's books; and the solicitor paid no more visits to Mrs Keepdown during the week leading up to the momentous birthday celebrations. So Jane decided to keep her own counsel for the present. which was just as well. Visor now lived in permanent dread of a telephone call or (worse) a personal visit from his daughter that would herald the betrayal of his sad secret, and the destruction of his peace of mind.

After a few days, he began to relax, but only slightly: at the back of his mind he feared that Kate would wait until the last possible minute to cause the trouble in which she delighted by revealing to Jane her paternity—on, perhaps, The Day itself, when such a story could only add to the general confusion. He guessed that it was only a matter of time before the unhappy truth of his love-life was common knowledge, and his tormented soul squirmed in the toils of his bleak, black imaginings.

There were no further visits from Dr Pickbone, either. Despite his warnings, Kate had rested quietly without having to be medically calmed: husbanding her strength, guessed the nurse, against the coming festivities. Every now and then she'd say: 'You wait and see how surprised they'll all be, after I'm gone!' or: 'I'll do what I please and they'll just have to lump it!' before a wicked chuckle; but she made no definite statements, seeming content to revel in the idea of chaos to come, so that it was a surprise to Jane when—

'I can't really trust any of 'em except you, girl, and I need you to look after me here,' announced Kate one day without warning. 'Just run down and tell 'em I want to talk to Stockfish, will you? *Will* you, hey? *Will* you?' And she burst out into her high-pitched, wheezing laugh.

Stockfish merely grunted when Susan passed on the message from Jane, and worked deliberately for another ten minutes before tidying himself sketchily and clumping his way up to Kate's bedroom where she waited, fully dressed, her swagger-stick across her knees. He stared expectantly at his bright-eyed employer, but, being now on her territory and not his, made no attempt to argue, standing in a gloomy, attentive silence until she deigned to address him.

'Now, see here, Stockfish,' she began. 'I want you to do an errand for me—today, because they'll all be arriving tomorrow. You must go into town and buy me—' she smirked sideways at Jane—'a packet of Will forms! I don't want just one, I'll need four, but there might be mistakes, so you'd better buy me six. Six Will forms, Stockfish—and where d'you think you're going, girl?' to Jane, who crossed to the door and was about to open it.

'If you're discussing your business in front of me, Mrs Keepdown, when you know I try not to listen to—'

'You stay here!' commanded Kate, while Stockfish maintained his habitual taciturn stance. 'You're my nurse, aren't you?'

Sighing, Jane returned, though it was clear from her expression that she deeply disapproved of her employer's careless and carefree behaviour. But—she ought not to annoy the old lady: Kate hated to be crossed, and Jane hated to upset a patient unnecessarily.

'Now *you*,' Kate triumphantly switched her attention to Stockfish, 'can leave right away—never mind what you're doing in the garden, it can wait. My business can't. Alice will give you some money, and you can take my bike, of course—but be careful with that machine, or I'll want to know all about it. Be off with you to buy those Will forms —bring 'em straight back, and don't waste time talking to anybody!'

This final sally set her laughing once more, while Stockfish nodded his assent and clumped away without a word. Jane looked anxiously towards her patient, now weakly giggling

—but Kate seemed brighter than she had done for a while, and the nurse decided no harm had been caused, except insofar as she herself had witnessed the entire scene. And when she said she disliked listening to gossip, being privy to other people's private affairs, she'd spoken the absolute truth . . .

There came a sudden series of loud banging pops, and a rattle like a small engine. Jane rushed to the window, to behold Sampson Stockfish inelegantly perched upon a solid little motor-bicycle, disappearing down the drive pursued by intermittent spurts of thudding, blue-grey smoke.

Kate crowed with delight. 'That's *my* motorbike, a Scott, the best they made when I was young. I was the first girl in the town with one, and I rode with the Club—they said it was only for men, but I joined all right, and I kept up with the front ones every time! Not that I've ridden it, since my accident—but things were made to last in those days, you know.'

'Surely it can't be safe? What about the brakes—just suppose a wheel came off, or the engine blew up—or—'

'Don't be a fool, girl! Just because *I* haven't ridden it for fifty years doesn't mean nobody else has. How did you think we kept in touch with the outside world when the railways don't run any more, and we don't have a car? Stockfish gets that bike overhauled every year at the garage, and the blacksmith makes the spare parts. It's quite a sight around the village, that crazy Stockfish doing the errands—but if he ever has an accident, I won't forgive him for smashing up my lovely Scott.'

Jane tried, in the ensuing pause, to envisage her employer as a spirited young woman defying convention to roar about the countryside on a motorbike; and looked with kindness on the plump, defiant old woman who sat dreaming before her, frail veined hands clasping the knob of the swagger-stick as she stared back into the past, and sighed.

'You mentioned an accident, Mrs Keepdown,' murmured Jane, as Kate awoke from her trance. 'On your motorbike?'

'Oh, I was still a young woman then, and so proud of my new machine. The Club was out for the first ride of spring, and of course, before we set out, they told me not to pass the captain—they always told me, it was against the rules, you see, and they fined you if you did—so I always passed him, it was part of the fun, and then I'd pay up and look big . . . This time, there was some young fellow who wanted to impress me with a bit of a race, and when we got round the corner after passing the captain, we didn't know there was flooding on the road—and we skidded into each other, and all the rest had been chasing us . . .

'Everybody came tumbling down on top of me and my bike—so I lost my baby, I was very ill, and we could never have another . . .' She sat up straight, a gleam in her eye. 'So that's why there's this fuss about my money now, with no real family to leave it to. Just you wait until that Stockfish comes back with my Will forms! Shall I tell you what I'm going to do?'

'I'd rather you didn't,' Jane interjected—unheeded.

'I'm going to make *four* Wills, all at the same time,' a slyly smiling Kate told her. 'And I'll leave it all to *each one of them*—and then, after the party, when they've chosen the best of the bunch—why, I'll burn the other three, and they can sort it all out from there!'

A steadily-increasing thud-pop-thud filled the air, and Kate stirred on the bed, blinking herself awake from the soothing nap Jane had prescribed. The nurse sat by the window, and confirmed the old lady's suggestion that Stockfish had returned. 'So now I'll start surprising 'em all!' gloated Kate, struggling to prop herself on her pillows to give a more impressive audience.

'Please don't excite yourself, Mrs Keepdown,' begged her harried attendant, hearing the clump of boots on the stairs. 'Are you sure you won't talk to Mr Visor again?'

'Visor—ha!' snapped Kate, to Jane's amazement. 'Talk to him—certainly not! You tell that Stockfish to come on in, and let's hear no more about my precious solicitor!'

Her vehemence so astonished Jane that the nurse forgot to utter her usual wish to forgo the proceedings: or did some imp of curiosity prompt her to remain? She watched Stockfish march across to the bed to offer Kate, without comment, a sturdy brown envelope which didn't crackle like an empty one. The old lady snatched at it, and shook the contents gleefully on the coverlet: out tumbled six individual documents of an official appearance. Kate turned them over in her gloating hands, and Jane saw that they were indeed those forms which can be bought at any stationer's, to save the purchaser the expense of consulting a member of the legal profession.

Kate's pleasure in Stockfish's bargain was so evident that he turned round and lurched away without waiting for dismissal. As soon as he'd slammed the door behind him, Kate spoke to Jane: 'Help me out of bed—quickly now— let me have a pen, and some ink—then you can leave me alone till I call you. I'm going to be busy for a while!'

Jane made no further attempt to expostulate, but did as she was asked, and in her turn went out of the door, closing it quietly on the small determined figure seated at the bed-side table, furiously writing. She wasn't recalled for some time; when she finally heard Kate's imperious bell, it summoned her to discover her charge admiring four pieces of stiff paper, each partly covered in Kate's still beautiful copperplate. The old lady brandished the forms triumphantly.

'D'you see here, girl? I told you I'd show 'em! Now I want you to fetch Stockfish up here again—nobody else will do—and then, I'm going to sign 'em. And you two must sign as well, and be witnesses! What are you waiting for?'

Jane hesitated, determined to try again. 'Won't you consider what you're doing, Mrs Keepdown? Wouldn't it be better to consult Mr Visor? I could just phone him—'

'No!' came the reply, swift and sharp. 'And if you knew about him what *I* know, you wouldn't be so happy to have

him handling people's affairs—affairs, ha! You just go along
and fetch me that Stockfish, will you?'

Jane went along, and fetched him. They stood near Kate
as she spread out the four Wills, though not close enough
to be able to read them; they watched as she signed them
one by one in the marked space; and, under her fierce
instruction, they signed after her. Stockfish wrote a round,
boardschool hand; Jane's, like herself, was neat and correct.
Kate blotted the documents, and folded them.

'I'll keep all of these until after my party,' she smiled,
'and then I'll burn all of 'em except one—I won't be
organized by other people into doing things their way and
not mine!' As she tucked the papers into her blouse front,
Stockfish stared mutely for a moment, then left. Jane sighed;
and jumped, as Kate snapped: 'Now then—what about my
lunch?' What had happened clearly didn't disturb her in the
least; and Jane resolved to behave with equal nonchalance, if
only she could.

The hearty meal Kate now expected caused an amusing
degree of inconvenience in the kitchen, so much later than
usual did she send for it; and afterwards, evidently more
tired by all the excitement than she would admit, she started
to nod. Jane helped her back on the bed, and left her to rest.

No sooner had the door closed than the old lady opened
a wideawake eye, raised herself on one elbow, and rolled
herself sideways to stand, rather shakily, on the floor. Sup-
ported by the furniture, she manœuvred her way round the
room to her dressing-table, where she opened one of the
small drawers flanking the mirror. It was not as deep as it
seemed: she fiddled about inside—there was a sudden, quiet
click—and the bottom lifted up, and out.

With a smirk, Kate took the four Wills from her bosom
and placed them carefully within the false bottom, where
other papers and a few photographs were already hidden.
She then replaced the gloves and handkerchiefs she'd previously removed, and stood, breathing hard, for a few
thoughtful minutes before taking herself back to bed. She

struggled in a clumsy scramble up against the pillows where
Jane had left her, then gave a quick gasp, followed by a
groan.

Within moments Jane was there. Her patient's appearance, although she tried not to show it, alarmed her: Kate
breathed fast and shallow, and her face looked grey. 'What
have you done, Mrs Keepdown, to get yourself in such a
state?' Jane demanded, as carefree as she dared, while she
took her pulse, feeling the skin clammy and cold—too cold.
'Let me make it easier for you,' she said, lifting the old lady
with one encircling arm while she removed all the pillows
with her free hand; she laid Kate flat on the bed, covered
her lightly with a blanket, and, with a reassuring whisper,
hurried from the room to the telephone.

As Dr Pickbone hastened to Kate's bedside, her relations
far and near were oblivious of her seizure, pursuing their
daily round untroubled. Henry was up a ladder in the
garden: having a day off work to make the most of the fine
late autumn weather, he was busy pruning trees. It was
unfortunate that his sense of balance didn't equal his enthusiasm: he leaned for a split second too far from the
perpendicular, fell with a clatter to the ground, and, landing
on his left arm, heard a sharp, crunching sound.

It was a strange coincidence that at almost the identical
moment, in the middle of the rose-bushes she was deadhead-
ing, Cicely tangled with a stubborn stem, which whiplashed
its displeasure against her own left arm, drawing blood and
sending her rushing into the house to bathe it.

Henry felt too sick and shocked to move. Luckily for him
Matthew (who'd taken some owed overtime to bone up on
that political literature demanded by his union activities)
heard the commotion: he jumped through the open sitting-
room window, and gently helped his friend to his feet. Henry
winced as he moved, and his left arm dangled useless by his
side.

'Hospital—casualty,' decided Matthew at once, and, as

Henry swayed and turned green, 'but brandy first—sit down
on the wall a minute . . .' He reappeared from the house
by a more conventional route, bearing a generously-filled
tumbler in one hand, and a wide square scarf in the other.
'I used to be a Boy Scout, before I realized they were
merely adjuncts to the class-conscious militarism of the
Establishment,' he said cheerfully, fashioning a rude sling.
'I'll try not to let it hurt too much—'

'My aunt!' groaned Henry, after a deep swig of spirit.

'I'm sorry—it was rather a long time ago, and we never
got the chance to practise on genuine invalids—'

'No, I didn't mean that. It hardly hurt at all,' Henry lied
bravely, thankful the worst was over. 'But this weekend it's
my aunt's birthday, and I'm meant to be helping to celebrate, as well as—the other business. How am I going to
get there if I can't drive?'

'Bus? Train?' suggested Matthew.

'No trains any longer,' said Henry sadly. 'And the buses
only run on one day a week—for the market in the
town . . .'

'Ask your cousin Gilbert for a lift.'

'If she *is* going to make her Will, I can't see *him* helping
another possible heir to turn up and cut him out—even
though he knows she can't stand him, or so she's always
made out—besides, he moves about such a lot, I wouldn't
know where to get hold of him to ask.'

'And you're right, anyway,' said Matthew, whose opinion
of Mr Peck wasn't high. 'He'd queer your pitch if he saw
even the slightest chance . . . Look, you know I don't
approve of capitalism, but, for a friend, I suppose I'd stretch
a point. How would it be if *I* drove you there?'

'Would you really?' At first, Henry was delighted, then:
'But—wouldn't it go against your principles?'

'To visit the house of a rich, sick, old woman? Not if I
thought I'd be helping you to your millions! Why, I might
manage to convert you to donate it all to the Cause!' He
chuckled. 'Some hopes . . . It'd be more likely that I'd bop

her over the head—euthanasia, you see . . . Sorry! Joke in
bad taste. Seriously, though, if you'd like me to, I'd be
happy to take you there.'

'Well, if you really would—thanks a lot, Matthew.'

He shrugged. 'What are friends for? Just remember me
when you come into your inheritance—if you ever do! Come
on, let's be off to the hospital.'

Cicely's scratch required no such drastic treatment, and
she sat on the kitchen stool quietly dripping blood into the
sink, feeling sick, and wishing Marian would come home.
Forgotten now was their quarrel of the morning: what did
it matter that they'd been unable to agree over whether they
ought to spend some of Marian's hard-earned money on a
present for Aunt Kate, or leave it to accrue yet more interest?

'Oh dear, I feel awful,' moaned poor Cicely, whose fair
skin was of that delicate sort which, once damaged, bruises
and bleeds alarmingly. 'At least it's not an artery—but I
do wish it would stop . . .'

'Talking to yourself is a bad habit,' scolded her sister,
who now appeared at the open kitchen door. 'And *you* have
no possible excuse—you aren't cooped up all day in that
ghastly school, trying to drive the least numerical ability
into the vapid brains of morons—oh, I see!'

In the silence which accompanied Marian's nimble ban-
daging of her sister's arm, no mention was made of the
quarrel. It was more important to set the home in order, for
sickness or weakness of any sort always displeased the elder
Miss Hacket by being so out of place. Just as the slipshod
work and untidy books of her pupils infuriated her, so did
such a change in her home routine, requiring them to buy
takeaway food or to eat out of tins, instead of enjoying
Cicely's fine cooking: not that it was the taste, or the fear of
additives, which annoyed Marian. It was the expense.

One decent killing on the Stock Exchange—one lump
sum with which to make that killing, and she'd be free of
this: the school, straitened means, maybe even—Cicely.
Marian supposed she cared for her quarter-century-younger

half-sister, but it wasn't in her cool, unfulfilled spinster's soul to care too deeply. And, away from Cicely, she'd feel free to exercise her keen financial brain without the underlying, confidence-lowering contrast of Cicely's gentle feminine presence always at hand.

Just one lump sum . . . 'I think you'll live now,' Marian encouraged her, tying the final flat reef-knot with a weary sigh. 'I'd better go out for something to eat, hadn't I? And —while I'm out, I'll—I'll buy Aunt Kate's present,' she promised wildly. The die was cast.

'It needn't cost much—it's the thought that counts. I mean, what could we give her that she couldn't buy for herself? She must be so very rich,' said innocent Cicely.

She missed the gleam in her sister's wild eye. 'It will be a fit and proper present for our only living relative,' Marian informed her haughtily; and was gone. Cicely sighed. She never seemed to say the right thing, where finance was concerned—she knew her sister dabbled in shares, but why was she always so sensitive about any mention of money, no matter how oblique? They must be much poorer than Cicely realized, and Marian was too kind to worry her about it . . . If only, mused Cicely, we had some money—if *I* had some, of course I'd share it with Marian . . .

For the thought came unbidden and tempting into her mind. She remembered Kate's quarrel with Marian, that dreadful day outside the eye-specialist's—the dislike towards her elder niece which Kate never troubled to hide. I wonder if—but Cicely stifled the rest of the sentence; although, she had no intention of turning down good luck—if it should happen to come her way . . .

At Swan House, Jane was wrestling with her conscience. As Dr Pickbone mixed his famous Cure-All, some faint memory had stirred within her—a long-ago recognition of scandal, of gossip about a breach of medical trust, which directly involved him. Nothing definite had been proved, she re-called, but general opinion had it that he was wise to resign his post at the big London hospital, and join his GP father in some quiet country practice . . .

Full recognition came to Jane when, in the middle of the night, she woke from the occasional nightmare about her own unhappy past, her tragedy and its drastic, desperate solution. Pickbone had performed an illegal operation on a student nurse, rather younger than Jane: complications had set in: the girl had died. Nobody could say for sure that Pickbone was the guilty party in either sense, for the pair had been discreet about their affair, the age difference and professional class distinction demanding secrecy; but he was much suspected. The party at which he'd mixed his Cure-All had been the final appearance before his ignominious retreat.

Jane, working at another hospital, had attended the party escorted by one able to whisper every detail of that pallid, exhausted body found in a grimly-stained room in the nurses' hostel . . . It was unlikely that Pickbone had recognized her after all this time, fleetingly glimpsed then if noticed at all, and dressed now, not informally, but in the protective disguise of the private nurse's uniform.

For Jane, too, wanted to shelter from the world: the risks she'd run, the life she'd destroyed, could still haunt her, both waking and sleeping. She needed to atone for what she'd done—and maybe Dr Pickbone felt the same. Should she then keep her own counsel, say nothing to Kate? When she thought of the way he'd laboured with her over the old lady, bringing her back with dedicated skill, she felt she could forgive him much—was she not also a sinner? But . . . there was always her duty to her patient, the strict and strait-laced, highly moral Kate Keepdown. Jane, after all, had betrayed only her heart; Pickbone had betrayed his professional trust . . .

The nurse rose, her mind made up, from her hard-backed chair, her rigorous training still forbidding her to sit on a bed. She was about to go to her patient's room, when her eye was caught by an unspecified lacuna on the bedside table: a few moments' thought showed her that her watch was missing. Not the sturdy, sensible, gunmetal timepiece, pinned as ever to her uniform; but her fine, dainty-braceleted wristwatch, the only present from the author of her misfortune she'd kept. He'd wined and dined her, shown her the high life, teased and adored her—before seducing her. The watch had been his attempt to change her image of herself into that sensuous and yielding creature he felt sure lay beneath her prim, vocational exterior.

'It's far too beautiful for me,' she exclaimed, admiring the small face, the sharp, clear dots instead of figures, the flickering moths' wings of the fragile hands.

'It's almost as beautiful as you are,' he assured her—and she'd believed him, trusted him.

But trust was betrayed, and shatteringly soon. 'You want me to marry you? I could never afford it! How could I support a wife and family? If you had money, that would be a different thing—but *I* certainly haven't! Never mind—you're a nurse, you'll know what to do.'

Even though he'd left her, she still cared—deeply, despite herself. And the watch was—had been—her only tangible reminder of him . . . Frantically, she searched: under the bed, behind the table, even flipping back the covers in case Susan, making the bed, had embroiled the precious watch among the clothes in her usual clumsy fashion.

It was nowhere to be found. And Jane's mind, unhinged by her disturbed night and resurrected memories, leaped to the one inescapable conclusion: Susan had stolen it.

'You're the only person who is supposed to go into that room, apart from myself,' she accused the startled Miss Grindstone a few moments later. 'You must have seen it!'

'Well, I haven't,' Susan assured her, reinforced in her pertness by the presence of Alice Shortcake.

'But it's not there—you *must* know where it is!'

'Susan don't tell lies,' snapped Alice. 'If she says she never saw it, then she never saw it—and you've got no call to come bursting into my kitchen saying such things. First it's the butler's books, then it's me—and now, if you like, you're saying as Susan's dishonest as well—it ain't right, and you ought to leave us all alone!'

Jane knew she'd gone too far: in her distress, she'd lost her head, panicked herself into wild accusations. She was unable to remain calm and rational, and the others could see that for themselves. Just as long as they maintained their united, stubborn, obstructive attitude, there wasn't anything she could now say or do to reach them; and, without another word, she left the room.

But she felt a murderous fury towards, not only Susan, but the entire domestic clan at Swan House.

And they felt almost as antagonistic towards her.

CHAPTER 5

Jane was too upset to dream of troubling her patient either with her suspicions of the staff or (more seriously) with those against the doctor: it was essential to regain her normal nurse's calm before she spoke. When Pickbone paid his final professional call on the afternoon of the birthday guests' arrival, she thought she'd managed it.

'Is anything wrong, Nurse?' inquired Dr Pickbone, after careful examination of Kate and nothing but praise for the way she'd survived that frightening attack: 'You'll live to get your telegram from the Queen, and I shall expect a bit of your celebration cake, shan't you, Nurse?'

Jane could only smile a frosty assent, without speaking: the thought had come to her that Kate's chances of seeing her hundredth birthday could be greatly affected by the events of the coming weekend: so many people might gain by her death in so many ways. How easy it would be to persuade an unscrupulous medical person to help her out of the world at the most convenient time! She knew little, not even the names, of the potential legatees—how did she know they could be trusted? As she knew, for sure, that Dr Pickbone, under certain temptations, could never be trusted . . .

And here he was, asking her what the matter might be. 'You're not ill, are you? Kate will need all the support she can commandeer for the next couple of days.'

'I'm perfectly well, thank you.' It was so unlike her not to use his title that he stared: but, in her eyes, he'd forfeited all right to it. 'Perhaps I just need to *a-ward myself a change of scene*, as my friends from St Agatha's used to say,' she suggested, and walked swiftly away.

The foolish pun from the past told him that the long arm of coincidence had finally reached him. Nursing could be, if you so wished, a peripatetic profession: not everyone stayed for life in the hospital where they'd trained—but, what damnably bad luck that someone who knew about him should come here, to nurse one of the most high-principled, upright old ladies for miles . . . a very sick old lady. Could he hope that a timely death would seal her lips, just as it had done for his victim, years ago? For once Kate knew, everybody would know: yet the nurse hadn't told her, he could tell from his patient's bright and jocular demeanour that afternoon . . . He heard Jane's swift footsteps behind him as he hesitated at the top of the stairs, and his chance was lost. She tapped on Kate's door and entered, opening the floodgates of scandal and ruin as she did so.

It was raining as he left Swan House, and the gloom of the overcast skies accorded well with his mood. Kate Keepdown was his greatest fear, he felt sure: the nurse would only speak out because it was a patient of hers who was involved. When she left, his secret would go with her: and he hoped they might never meet again. But the lady of the manor, with her strong sense of right and wrong, her duty to the village—she would remain, as he must do—for where else could he go, always running the risk of meeting someone else who might recognize him? He was helpless, at her mercy . . . And, as he drove down the drive, overhung by trees moisture-drooping above his car, his thoughts, like the raindrops thudding on the roof, were heavy.

He passed another car coming up the drive, headlights full on and its driver slow to respond to his impatient flashings. Henry Pimpernell, chauffeured by the ebullient Matthew Goffe, had arrived.

He'd telephoned ahead to ask if, given his incapacity, he might be brought by a friend; and if said friend could stay as well. Kate relayed her grudging acceptance of an extra visitor, and Alice aired another bed. Henry also called a motoring organization, as most prudent long-distance drivers do, to inquire what the journey might have for them in the way of weather.

'Absolutely filthy,' he was advised in the cheerful tones of one who doesn't have to travel far. 'Strong winds, low cloud cover, and it'll be raining stair-rods all the way. I'd stay at home, if I were you.'

Could this be the voice of Fate, showing signs of precognitory conscience, disliking the idea of a life cut short by murder? If it was, Henry had ignored it, and now climbed the well-known steps to ring the bell without a qualm.

Hour, his eyes red-rimmed (a cold? a hangover?), came to meet them in the hall, with Alice not far behind.

'Mr Henry—after all this time! And how kind of you to bring him, Mr Er, with his poor arm all broke as it is— would you like me to look at it, Mr Henry?'

'No, thank you,' shuddered Henry, recalling past horrific herbal cures she'd tried on him in his youth. 'I'm fine.'

'Missus is resting for now, but she'd like to see you a bit later—so you make yourselves comfortable, and ring for Susan if you need anything.' She sketched something like a curtsey, bobbing deferentially, and left them.

Mr Goffe muttered concerning *downtrodden serfs* and *the feudal system* as he helped Henry unpack, but expressed himself no more forcibly until his friend, banging on the dividing wall, demanded assistance in buttoning a clean shirt, which he felt the great Audience would require.

'What d'you think of the place?' asked Henry, as Matthew stood behind him, trying to knot his tie. 'Not bad, eh?'

'Not bad, no,' grinned Matthew. 'Absolutely terrible is more the word—it's an anachronism, it's mediaeval—all that kowtowing and scraping, calling you *Mr Henry* and asking you to ring for whatever you need—what a waste! An entire houseload of people slaving away to look after just one person—doesn't that seem wrong to you?'

'You're looking after just one person right now,' Henry pointed out, returning his grin. 'Thanks for the tie!'

'But you *need* help, mine or someone else's, don't you? You're not simply expecting to batten on other people as your birthright. To each according to his needs . . .'

'Maybe they all *need* my aunt,' suggested Henry, with some of Kate's own mischief in his voice. 'If she stopped them working for her—if she sacked them, threw them out —what would they do, and where would they go? They could've left here any time in the last hundred years or so, but they've chosen to stay—and they seem perfectly happy —so don't they have the right to choose whether to be exploited, or whatever it is you think's happening here?'

'Brainwashing,' countered Matthew, dusting a few specks off his friend's shoulder. 'The poor things don't know any better . . . When I'm honoured with admission to the glorious presence of your dear great-aunt, I'm going to say *Greetings, Comrade!* just to see how she reacts.'

'How can you call her a comrade when you've said she's a capitalist exploiter of the downtrodden proletariat?'

'D'you want me to tighten the knot on your tie for you?' threatened Matthew, as Henry chuckled; but his onslaught was interrupted by a tap at the door.

'Are you ready to come to the missus now, Mr Henry?' And Susan Grindstone led him to Kate's bedroom.

The young revolutionary, abandoned, wandered downstairs, to witness an amusing commotion in the hall: Gilbert Peck had arrived, and, like Henry, not alone. Unlike Henry, his companion was (a) unexpected and (b) female—decidedly so. Perigenia had refused to let Gilbert go without her, and, fearing one of her ferocious and jealous scenes, he had weakly agreed that she should come.

Her sultry presence had completely overwhelmed an already confused Hour, who shambled into the kitchen to fetch his sister. They conferred in disapproving whispers over what to do with her: no other rooms were aired, ready, or suitable—yet she looked unlikely to leave without her reluctant, besotted escort. The twins were arguing the merits of (a) leaving the stranger to freeze to a wanton's death ('With hair like that, she's no better than she should be!') in the damp, unused wing, or (b) placing her, morals notwithstanding, with Mr Peck.

Throughout this confabulation, the immodest pair waited in the hall. Gilbert's temper was slowly mounting, while Perigenia prowled the room to admire the various old and choice items with which it was furnished; there were hunting prints on the walls, together with the essential decorative weaponry of a country house where a murder is shortly to take place: poniards, dudgeons, misericordes, stylets; calivers, arquebuses, petronels, and escopettes. There was also a large carved wooden chest at the foot of the stairs, and a dark oak settle, lion-armed and serpent-backed, nearby. Upon this last the film star, instantly recognizable to an appreciative Matthew, eventually sat, and began a sulky complaint that she was tired from the journey.

Mr Goffe decided to join the merry throng, and strolled with maddening nonchalance to greet Gilbert. 'Better late than never, eh, Peck? Ghastly weather for a long trip.'

Gilbert scowled at the unexpected welcome. He was cold, and tired (partly from the journey, partly from the nightly exertions demanded of him by Perigenia), and would have liked a friendly whisky, with polite inquiries after his well-being. Instead, he'd been kept hanging about in a chilly hall by a couple of mindless prudes—and here was that damned Red pal of his fool cousin Henry, wandering about as if he owned the place.

'What in thunder are you doing here, Goffe? I thought it was supposed to be for family only.'

'Oh, really?' Matthew cocked a quizzical eyebrow in the direction of Perigenia. 'Yes, well, in *my* case, there's a special dispensation—Henry's broken his arm, so I had to drive him. I gather that you—er—forgot to let them know you'd be bringing company?'

'Bloody cheek!' cried Gilbert, though nobody knew if he meant it for Matthew or the whisperers. His outburst had the advantage of rousing Alice Shortcake to a decision, for she waddled upstairs, muttering about having to find another room; Hour, reminded of his butlerial obligations, took Gilbert's coat and directed him towards the sitting-room. He completely ignored Perigenia.

'If you want a drink, Mr Gilbert, Mr Goffe—there's some over there,' waving towards the silver tray. 'I'll be sending Susan in with some ice for you later.'

'*Ice?*' Gilbert was horrified. 'In weather like this? Are you completely mad?'

'I'd like ice in mine, darling,' purred Perigenia, who hated being neglected. The loving epithet she addressed to Gilbert meant, in these circumstances, quite the opposite: she thought he should have stood up more on her behalf against the servants, for Perigenia liked her men to be—well, manly, in every sense. 'I'm so hot-blooded, I need all the cooling-down I can get.' And she smirked provocatively towards Mr Goffe, who goggled in surprise.

'Matthew Goffe is a friend of my cousin Henry,' Gilbert introduced them casually, assuming that Matthew would know, without explanation, who she was; Mr Peck was working up his own temper into something heated.

Mr Goffe guessed that the coming weekend wouldn't be without its points of interest. If he accepted the petulant Perigenia's clear invitation to flirt, it would annoy Gilbert: since the two men had nothing in common beyond mutual acquaintance with Henry, and disliked each other, Mr Goffe would enjoy making Mr Peck cross. There was also Henry to consider: was his great-aunt the severely moral type who'd so deplore Gilbert's wench that she'd disinherit him at first sight of those voluptuous curves and that brazen hair?

On the other hand: if Matthew flirted with the actress, the old lady might be pleased with Peck for having managed to off-load his troublesome partner, and Henry would find his nose out of joint as she smiled upon her elder heir . . . and what about the female cousins Henry had mentioned? What were they likely to make of it all?

As he faded his smile into a mere social response, Perigenia's red lips twisted into a pout; and there came a loud and sudden tattoo upon the doorknocker. Mr Goffe was about to discover what the Hackets would make of it all.

Marian had rapped with such insistence: for Marian was very angry. Cicely, being totally unsuited to driving, had never learned; map-reading, therefore, fell to her as a fair division of labour. Unfortunately, with the bad weather's delays, her sister had been tempted to speed, when the rare chance presented itself; Cicely, no robust traveller, felt sick —and missed a vital turning—so they had got lost, to arrive much later than they'd planned.

Marian's temper wasn't improved by the news that she and Cicely must share a room. Alice chose to solve the problem of Perigenia by giving her the room originally meant for Cicely, at the far end of the corridor, well away from whatever Gilbert might design. Cicely would now share the next-door chamber with Marian, the other side to Kate; Gilbert was directly opposite the nurse, with Mr Pimpernell and Mr Goffe next in order. Decorous whitewash thus having been applied, some necessary furniture-shifting was going on above everyone's heads as the newcomers were ushered in.

Hour wasn't sure how to announce them (if at all): *the Miss Hackets, the Misses Hacket,* or *Miss Marian and Miss Cicely Hacket?* In the end, he opened the door and said to the

sisters, 'Mr Henry's just gone in, and he's got a friend with
him—Mr Gilbert's there, too.' Then he shut the door behind
them, and shuffled, duty done, back to his lair—leaving the
relations all staring at one another.

Down in Bardleton village, Quentin Lees, having made his
way through storm and flood, had settled for a lazy, cosy
chat with *his* relation, Miss Ellen Silence.

'Being promoted suits you,' Great-Aunt Ellen informed
him, her eyes twinkling.

'And moving house seems to suit you! You look far better
for the change—it's time you had a place with central
heating and not too many rooms to look after.'

'Your cousin Bridget's been wonderful, the way she's got
things organized—even the painting. Can you smell it?'

'Don't worry, the spare room's fine—and everywhere else
looks fine too. You included!'

'But not poor Pooter,' sighed Aunt Ellen. 'I suppose it's
the paint that makes him sulk so, though it may be the
different climate—he did enjoy the sea air, you see. Or
maybe he's tired of living with me, and wants a change.'

'Talking of changes—' Lees hated to see the old lady, of
whom he was very fond, despondent—it wasn't at all like
her—'do you think that *I* ought to change?'

She looked at him in amazement. 'What! When you're
the youngest superintendent in the county? Whatever
would you want to do that for?'

'Oh, not change my job, but myself. Perhaps I should
have a hobby—grow orchids, or vegetable marrows—'

'You, gardening? Don't make me laugh. Besides, you're
nowhere near fat enough to grow orchids.'

Lees stretched his spare six-foot-three frame luxuriously
in the low armchair, and grinned. 'Well, I could keep bees,
I suppose—I could always sell the honey.'

'If you got any! And bees sting, remember? I'd leave well
alone, if I were you.'

'Then should I cultivate an urbane and polysyllabic con-

versational style, and involve myself in only the most erudite
and uncommonly freakish undertakings?'

Aunt Ellen merely looked at him—hard.

He shrugged. 'Oh well, it was just an idea.'

'What about Pooter?' she said, after a thoughtful pause.

'What *about* Pooter?'

'I told you he hasn't been happy since we moved here—
not his usual self at all. And I'm getting old. Really, he
needs lively young company, like you—and you wouldn't
have to take him for walks, or anything. Your odd hours
wouldn't bother him—and,' Miss Silence said above her
great-nephew's protest, 'you might even be able to get him
to talk!'

They both studied the bright green parrot on his perch,
a stubborn look in his beady eye. 'It's a proper mystery,
why he's never said anything,' sighed his owner. 'If you
talked some sense into him, it would be a miracle—as well
as giving you something unusual for a hobby.'

'Talking of talk—' Lees changed the subject, to let his
subconscious work on her suggestion—'what about all this
village gossip you promised me? Scandal and rumour and
I don't know what, your letter said—so come on, out with
it!'

Which explains why (Bardleton being what it was) he
soon knew almost as much about the goings-on at Swan
House as anybody within those walls could possibly do.

The Hacket sisters had met their relatives by marriage on
few occasions, but enough to be able to greet them with an
air of familiarity; on Cicely's part, that is. She was glad to
see Cousin Henry again, although Gilbert had never been
one of her favourite people. Marian, whose quicker mind
saw trouble ahead, merely nodded round the room, lifted
an eyebrow at Perigenia, and went across to the fire, where
she stood warming her hands.

Cicely accepted a small glass of sherry, and Henry introduced Matthew, with an explanation of his presence. Gilbert

(who'd attempted to gloss over the presence of *his* guest) almost audibly ground his teeth. Perigenia still sulked in a corner, undecided how best to play her role.

Henry's splint was a conversational ice-breaker. Matthew made Cicely giggle, and even Marian grimly smile, with his highly-coloured account of the rescue dash to the hospital, and Henry's sufferings in the Casualty Ward.

'Oh dear, what a shame! We shouldn't laugh, poor you,' sympathized Cicely, her eyes sparkling. Henry smiled back into their friendly grey depths.

'Oh, I don't mind now. The worst of it's over—just a spot of inconvenience left really, I suppose.'

'I even have to knot his tie for him,' chuckled Matthew, remembering just in time that the buttoning of shirts might be a little indelicate for present company. 'By the way, Henry—how did it go, when you saw the old lady?'

This casually-dropped bombshell alerted Gilbert and Marian at once. Only sweet Cicely thought nothing of it, and asked immediately, 'Oh, have you seen Aunt Kate already? How is she? Can she walk properly yet?'

Before he could reply, Perigenia decided that the time was ripe for her reappearance. 'Gilbert, darling, will our rooms be ready now? I'm simply longing to change after that ghastly journey, and soak in a hot tub.'

Her strident demands drove everything else from his head, for here, in the house of his well-respected aunt, in the presence of his relations, he was unable to brazen things out the way he could on his own ground. 'Let's go and find out,' he muttered, beckoning her to come with him and, as she delayed to make a performance out of it, seizing her by the wrist. 'Hurry up—if you're so cold!'

'I'm such a hot-blooded person *usually*,' everyone heard her enunciating as he closed the door behind them; and the room she had so noticeably left seemed to shake itself back to normal. She'd been as out-of-place in it as a hornet in a Horlicks jar.

'Come, Cicely—' Marian spoke more stiffly than in-

tended, and her sister gave a guilty start—'shall we find
out what *our* sleeping arrangements are?' For Perigenia's
remarks had reminded her that she and Cicely were to share
a room, and she was still not resigned to it.

As they passed through the door, Sir Bennet Seely entered
in a blast of cold air from the dark outside. Matthew (as
Henry's disability prevented his playing host) helped the
little baronet to a drink; Henry was an old, if distant,
acquaintance, and a general (though muted) conversation
ensued. When, shortly after, Dr Pickbone and Mr Visor
arrived together, it became almost lively: Pickbone showed
professional interest in Mr Pimpernell's injured limb, while
Matthew joined in a discussion between Visor and Seely
about fishing rights on the River Avon, throwing in the odd
controversial remark to keep things going.

For, despite the semblance of a normal party, everybody
felt the underlying tension. As first Gilbert, then the two
Hackets, returned, people began looking at their watches—
surreptitiously wondering how long they must wait to greet
their hostess, that as yet unseen, omnipotent old lady. Now
Visor and Pickbone feared her; Gilbert and Marian, knowing she disliked them, wished to propitiate her; Seely had
cared little for her ever since she ran off with his sister's
intended. Cicely was rather scared of her, while Henry
(who'd had that strange audience with her) believed she
was plotting mischief. Even Matthew, bold revolutionary
though he was, couldn't help wondering . . .

In her room, Kate deliberated over what to wear with a
vanity that would have amazed Perigenia. Too old, too
dingy, not enough fullness for her to walk in—she threw
down dress after dress, and drove Jane wild.

'And I won't sit myself in that fancy wheelchair you've
gone and borrowed, indeed I won't,' she informed the nurse,
as she was buttoned into the garment of her final choice.
'We'll get Alice Shortcake to help you take me downstairs,
and I'll have my swagger-stick with me—and you'll be there
too, of course, all evening, won't you?'

'Oh,' said Jane. 'Mrs Keepdown—I beg your pardon, but—naturally, if you need me at any time, you have only to call me. But please—don't ask me to be in the same room as Dr Pickbone—it would—it would seem too much like—like condoning a murder.'

'Ah, yes.' Kate nodded, as Jane shivered; for now the truth had been told, and Pickbone's secret was ready to be disclosed as and when his despotic patient thought fit. She had condemned the story with withering curtness: 'No moral fibre! He should have stood by her—people who panic like that don't have the courage of their convictions, not standing by the results of their actions—weak-willed, the way too many people are today. Don't tell me it was all a long time ago, people don't change as they grow older. If you've panicked once, you'll do it again. Well, he's another one I'll have nothing more to do with after this weekend!'

Jane sighed, for she'd regarded Visor (whom she guessed was also to be rejected) as a distant avuncular friend for most of her life; and some of Kate's remarks about him had been very scathing. The old lady misunderstood her emotion.

'Cheer up, girl! It was your duty to tell me, and you should be proud of yourself. Looking miserable won't help, you know—and if you perked up a bit, you could be almost pretty, dressed smartly, with your hair done.'

Jane had to smile as her hand went automatically to the smooth honey-blonde pleat of hair beneath her prim cap: it had been kindly meant, and she was grateful. But—*almost pretty*, when one person, one only, had called her beautiful —had life drained her of so much indeed?

As Alice came in answer to her bell, Kate issued final instructions. 'Make sure this door's properly shut, won't you? There's papers hidden away here that quite a few folk in this house would love to have a look at, I know!'

'Mrs Keepdown, really—' Jane began her warning.

'Oh, hush! If I can't trust Shortcake and the others, after all the years they've worked for me—why, then I can't trust anyone!' Jane's eyes briefly met Alice's hostile gaze, then looked away. 'It's those precious relatives of mine I have to watch, you know. I don't want anybody to be surprised until after I'm gone—they'll have to mind their own business till then, like everyone else!'

The trio made its careful way down the stairs, Kate gripping Jane's supportive arm and placing her feet in steady rhythm upon tread after tread; at the bottom, she paused for breath. Silently, Alice left them; Jane watched her go, now sure that she'd been right not to mention to Kate her suspicions of the staff. Let the old lady keep her illusions! If she was about to be surrounded by crowds of relations all (apparently) hungry for money, she had to be able to trust as many people as possible. But Jane remembered that desperate wish for money in her own sad dilemma —how she would then have been able to keep him, would never have had to—

'I'll go straight to the dining-room, if you please,' a panting Kate broke in on her bleak thoughts. 'Then they can come in to see me—I don't want the lot of 'em drinking at my expense all night. You get me settled, then go and tell Hour to fetch 'em all in. You can ask Alice to send something up for you on a tray, if you like.'

She wasn't usually so thoughtful for others: no doubt the excitement of anticipation had mellowed her. As Jane went into the kitchen to look for Hour, she passed the sitting-room door, and heard snatches of conversation, a babble of strange voices. How quickly would they fall quiet, once Hour had announced their hostess's invitation?

He was in the kitchen with the others, talking in muted accents which mumbled immediately into a sinister silence at her approach. So hostile was the atmosphere that she could hardly bring herself to deliver her message: six glaring eyes, dark with dislike, rendered her dumb.

'What did you want? asked Alice Shortcake in a voice that dripped venom. Jane managed to gasp out Kate's orders to Hour, but never dared to mention that *something sent up on a tray* to his sister.

'Oh, and by the by—' Alice arrested her as she turned to leave. 'Susan found your watch this morning while she was sweeping the stairs. Here you be.' She put it down on the table, and pushed it disdainfully towards Jane, who felt her legs strangely shaky as she stepped forward to pick it up. Her tongue wouldn't, couldn't, frame words of thanks: the slug-slimy touch of the housekeeper was almost tangible about the precious watch. She nodded to Susan, and left the room without another word.

Did they hate her, then, so much—making her wait for its return so long, tormenting her, paying her back for those unjust but frantic accusations she'd made? Now, she could reason that, in Susan's case, she might have been wrong— during that anguished, restless night, she'd gone downstairs to heat herself some milk, and donned her dressing-gown: a long, sweeping garment which could easily have caught in the fine filigree of the bracelet. At least the watch wasn't broken—she'd been spared that, for, even if the fall had not damaged it, the servants might have done something, out of spite . . . and she would starve, rather than let Alice prepare her a tray to eat upstairs, alone. In the city she would have laughed at herself, having such fears of the housekeeper's rumoured witch-hood: in the country isolation of Swan House, such fears were only too real.

Perigenia passed her on the stairs, rustling in an exotic full-length gown more honoured in the breach than in the observance. Jane wondered what could have brought such a woman here: there had been a passionate look in the emerald eyes that crossed briefly with her own steady blue ones—something wild and unstable. Drink, maybe, or drugs —a strange guest indeed for the upright Mrs Keepdown.

Hour opened the sitting-room door; Perigenia caught the buzz of conversation, the opportunity for a drink. And how badly she needed one! Instead of the wealthy country house she'd expected, Gilbert had brought her to a mausoleum with antiquated plumbing (she grimaced) and a total lack of lively company—that company her jealous mind had envisaged as female, and interested in Gilbert. She would have done far better to have believed him about the dullness of his duty visit, and stayed back in Town . . . but at least she'd fixed herself up before coming to join this party, boring as it was. Gilbert still believed that those anonymous white tablets were birth control pills . . .

Thinking of Gilbert, she saw him. The guests were now crossing the passage in response to Hour's summons; Gilbert, closing his eyes at the sight of Perigenia's daring attire and wishing he'd warned her, beckoned her to join him. Too late to send her to change—better get it over with . . . So, together, following the others, the pair advanced into the lioness's dining-room den.

CHAPTER 6

Everyone muttered a greeting of some sort as they entered, and Kate, sitting still and stately on her chair, held them for a long moment with a glittering eye. It was Henry upon whom she first smiled: she may have quarrelled with his forebears, but at least he'd done her the courtesy of arriving on time.

She beckoned him forward. 'Introduce me to your friend, young man. Malcolm Croft, isn't it?'

'Matthew Goffe,' the newly-named informed her as he shook hands, ignoring Henry's meaningful look. He was determined that this formidable old lady wasn't going to bully *him* as she seemed to do with everybody else.

She twinkled her bright black-eyed gaze at him, pleased. 'Well, young Matthew, if it wasn't for you, Henry wouldn't be here, would he? He should be very grateful to you, very grateful indeed.' She paused wickedly to give her words a sinister emphasis before continuing: 'But in *my* day, a man who couldn't do a simple thing like prune a tree without tipping himself off a ladder wasn't worth much at all!' Thus having demolished any hopes Henry might have permitted himself, she returned to Matthew. 'You're a revolutionary of sorts, I'm told. Is that so?'

'I suppose some people might call me that,' he agreed.

'But would you?' she cried, thumping her heavy stick on the floor. 'I can't bear people who don't speak out—makes me think they don't know their own minds.'

'If a revolutionary is someone dedicated to changing life for the better, then yes, I am—but,' Matthew found himself promising, 'I won't guillotine *you*, Mrs Keepdown, when the great day comes. It would be a real pity to do that!'

'*I* shan't live to see any such thing,' she sniffed. 'Oh, there's been talk of revolution ever since I was a girl, but nothing ever comes of it. Mind you, that was a pretty compliment you paid me, and I appreciate it. I dare say Henry here put you up to it, but I still appreciate it.'

'Aunt Kate, really—' began Henry, but she frowned at him.

'Ha! Never mind, never mind . . . You shall sit next to me at supper, Matthew, and tell me all about your precious revolution—and you can teach me the words of *The Red Flag* as well.' She chuckled at his stare of surprise.

Her own flesh and blood had been fidgeting, ignored, in the background during this exchange, and she switched her attention to her nieces rather suddenly.

'So here you both are, come all this way to wish a happy birthday to your poor, lonely old aunt! Well—' as they both began to speak, and stopped in confusion—'aren't you even going to kiss me, and ask me how I am?'

'We can see for ourselves how well you're keeping, Aunt Kate,' Marian assured her, wishing her hands didn't feel so awkward and in the way. 'And—thank you for asking us to come,' she faltered, her nerve crumbling at the thought of the salutation Kate had demanded. Surely it would choke her to dance attendance on this cantankerous old woman? But—this cantankerous, *rich* old woman . . .

Cicely, from the kindness of her heart, got there first.

'You're looking very well, Aunt Kate.' And her aunt smiled with genuine pleasure at the lovingly tentative peck on her soft rose-water cheek, and nodded her approval.

Marian was spared her ordeal by Kate's next attack. 'I know who *you* are, sir, don't I? But I don't remember,' she said icily to Gilbert, 'inviting anyone else with you. Who is that? Come over here, and let me see you properly.'

Reluctantly, they approached the judgement seat. The firelight cast deep shadows into Perigenia's cleavage; Kate sniffed, and pursed her lips.

'You must be extremely cold in that dress,' she dismissed her, and to Peck: 'So *you've* turned out no better and no worse than I expected! Well, every family has its black sheep, sir, but I've agreed to treat you all quite fairly—perfectly fairly, no matter what I think!' Once more, she thumped the swagger-stick on the ground. 'So let's be getting on with things now we're all here, shall we?'

The three Judges looked at one another, each waiting for somebody else to speak. Pickbone and Visor, both afraid of antagonizing her, were uncertain how to begin: it was left to Sir Bennet, in the end. After all, *noblesse oblige.*

'I wonder, Mrs Keepdown, if any of the members of your family have any idea of, er, the true purpose in your asking them to visit you this weekend?' And he looked towards the solicitor for a lead, as Kate grimaced in silence; Mr Visor gulped, and struggled to hide his distaste.

'Unless Mrs Keepdown has added anything to the letter of invitation which I drew up according to her specifications, subsequent to my sending of it to all four persons directly involved and present here tonight—no.'

'Then perhaps it would be in order for everyone to sit down?' suggested Seely, knowing that it is harder to stay angry when physically comfortable. Kate waved her hand in the direction of the mahogany table, but herself remained apart, a plump silhouette in the firelight. Matthew, after a quick check with Henry, placed himself beside her, out of the way of the family, who settled themselves in some bewilderment; Perigenia, having snatched and drained Gilbert's glass, posed herself (completely ignored by her hostess) on the other side of the fireplace. An expectant hush fell.

Seely cleared his throat. 'Maybe it would be better if, er, only those members of Mrs Keepdown's family and others, er, directly involved, were to attend this discussion?'

At once Perigenia seized the chance to be the centre of attention. 'But of course, if anything private's going on, we simply must leave! If I'd only known, I'd never have come here making a nuisance of myself, would I, darling?' Gilbert winced. 'I'm sure Matthew and I could be perfectly happy waiting together somewhere else, couldn't we?'

Matthew recoiled, and Kate saved her *cavalier servente* at once, by commanding him to stay put. 'It won't do us any harm to have an independent witness, will it? Even if he's a revolutionary . . . So let's get on with it, do!'

Sir Bennet sighed; hesitated; made a couple of false starts; and then, beneath Kate's stare, explained her plan.

The silence which followed his laboured and embarrassed exposition was stunned. Then Marian and Gilbert burst into wild expostulation, while Cicely, trying to take it all in, met Henry's friendly, amused gaze, and felt better.

Gilbert's louder voice prevailed. 'My dear Aunt Kate, I wonder at your suggesting such a crazy scheme. Surely there can be no question of *my* right to inherit? As the eldest Keepdown heir, that is. I know Uncle Luke left no Will— but surely the logical person—'

'Nonsense!' snapped Kate. 'There are no male Keepdowns of the name left, you're only the son of his sister— while Henry here—' fomenting trouble with every syllable —'is descended from a male Keepdown, his grandfather. Maybe you'll say I ought to leave it all to Henry, then?'

'But, Aunt Kate,' interposed Marian, 'Cicely and I aren't just connections by marriage, but your own flesh and blood. And I, of course, am the elder.'

'You've only your parents to thank for that, miss,' Kate

sharply informed her. 'Cicely is just as much my niece as
ever you could be—aren't you, hey?'

'Well—but, Aunt Kate, Marian and I share everything,
you see, because we live together,' blushed Cicely.

'So she writes to me every few weeks exactly the same as
you do, does she? Nice newsy letters, take time to scribble
a few lines to your poor lonely old aunt . . .'

'I sign them from both of us,' Cicely dared to protest on
her sister's behalf. 'Marian's busy—she works.'

'And that's why they're the same handwriting all the way
through!' crowed Kate, feeling she'd scored.

Indeed she had, for from the Hackets there came nothing
more. Matthew, fervent socialist, attempted to intervene.
'If you really don't mind which one you leave whatever-it-is
to, why not leave it in four equal shares? Surely that's by
far the fairest way of doing it!'   •

'It's not good for property to be chopped into pieces,' Kate
loftily advised the whole room. 'I have a trust—my lawful
inheritance to pass on. Things have to continue as they've
always done, with Keepdowns in the manor on this side of
the river, and Seelys over the way—even if the name's gone,
the inheritance is still there, isn't it?'

Gilbert appealed to Pickbone in a low voice. 'Can she be
mentally sound, do you think, to suggest such an idea?'

The doctor flinched. At all costs, he must keep on the
right side of his patient, now that he knew *she* knew: not
once had she looked at him since he came into the room.
He could hardly tell Peck she was off her head—yet an
impartial observer, a stranger to her eccentricities, might
find it credible—and so might a court of law . . .

'I'm not deaf,' Kate told her nephew, 'and I'm not daft,
either—in fact, my mental state must be far better than
yours—bringing a wanton woman to a decent household,
flaunting her about the place. You ought to be downright
ashamed of yourselves, both of you!'

This was too much for Perigenia. 'How dare you! Who
are you to call me names, you rude old hag? Gilbert, make

her apologize! Ever since I arrived she's looked at me as if I was dirt, and never even bothered to say Hello—if this is your fine family weekend, you can keep it!'

'It was my nephew to whom the invitation was addressed,' returned Kate. 'Certainly not his—lady friend. Besides, this is none of your business, my girl, none at all.'

Even as Gilbert muttered to her to forget it, Perigenia flared up. Boredom, drugs and drink had combined to make her fighting angry: she shouted at Gilbert, yelled at Kate, and then bounded to the table to snatch up a wicked-looking carving knife. 'Say you're sorry, you rude old witch!' she cried. Gilbert leaped to his feet, but Kate, unruffled, was equal to the situation. She leaned calmly over to where a stunned Matthew was still sitting, and remarked:

'Just ring that bell there, would you? We'll get Hour to throw a bucket of cold water over her. In my young day it was the proper treatment for hysterics.'

'Allow me,' said Matthew with pleasure, rising to his feet and hurrying over to a large jug full of late chrysanthemums. He laid the flowers on a side table, picked up the jug, and tipped the contents over the now screeching actress's head, to Kate's evident glee. Perigenia gasped, squealed, dropped the knife, and jumped at Matthew; he took a step backwards; Gilbert came to his senses and seized her by the arms from behind. She wriggled furiously in his clutch, spitting out scurrilities in all directions; he shook her hard, so that her eyes popped and her hair tumbled down, but she managed to break away from him, just as the door opened.

'Hour,' said Kate, who'd summoned him herself after Matthew took matters into his own hands, 'here is a lunatic. Kindly arrange for Nurse to deal with her.'

'All right.' Years of service with Kate Keepdown had left him surprised by little; dripping, dishevelled women in scanty gowns might have been all in a normal day's work, from the easy way he seized Perigenia's arm in a huge fist, and made to frogmarch her to the door.

Matthew detained him, holding out the pottery jug: 'We'll

need some more water for the flowers—d'you think you could fix it when you come back, please?'

'I'll send Susan,' said Hour, as Perigenia swore at her tormentors. The strange pair left, and Matthew returned to his seat by the old lady, who smiled at him before addressing Gilbert in an icy tone.

'Nice goings-on! Loose women in my house, screaming and screeching—what fine company you choose to keep, sir!'

Gilbert could quite cheerfully have strangled both Perigenia and Kate for putting him in such a spot. He tried to bluster some excuse, but his aunt interrupted him.

'Well, I heard what he said to you—' turning to Pickbone —'and you can see for yourself, can't you, that it isn't me who's the crazy one around here . . . can't you?'

'So far as I can tell, there is nothing wrong with your aunt's mental state,' he advised everyone, his heart thudding. 'She's always been—strong-minded, some might say eccentric, but there can be no doubt at all of her sanity.'

'Oh, good try, Francis!' she applauded. 'But you won't make me change my mind, you know.' Everybody else thought she must be speaking of her Will—but Pickbone was the only one who knew for certain that she wasn't.

Roused from her solitude by the rumpus, Jane met Hour, half way up the stairs, bear-leading Perigenia, whom he shoved towards the nurse with brief and mumbled instructions. Jane was left alone with her damp, distraught captive. Perigenia shook with more than cold, judged the nurse; but first, she must be made dry, and put to bed. Only then might it be possible to learn what she'd taken to excite her so.

There was a long mirror in Perigenia's room, fixed to a wardrobe opposite the door: as Jane, her arm about her, came face to face with their joint reflection, even she was surprised. 'Look,' giggled the actress. 'Snap!'

For so it was, at a quick glance in the dimly-lit room: both tall and slim, both blonde, but one blue-eyed and calm, the other with an erratic emerald gaze. Jane smiled briefly, and helped her charge over to the bed. Perigenia, still giggling, lay down; Jane covered her with a blanket after stripping her of her wet clothes, then disappeared into the bathroom to mix an emetic.

She returned to a monotone complaint that the actress had not come here to be insulted, that they were all against her, that the warm salty water tasted awful and was part of some plot to poison her, and that Gilbert ought to have stood up for her better against his wicked old aunt.

Jane froze in the very act of coaxing down more salt-and-warm-water. Surely, after all this time—it couldn't be!

'Mr Popular Peck, the ladies' man, can't even keep one old witch quiet—so, yes, he's good in bed, but what's the use of that? Some hero, letting them all insult me!'

Jane's face was whiter than her uniform cuffs, her eyes opaque glass set in granite. It was—she'd found him! The misery, the years of lonely waiting were forgotten: she was under the same roof as her lost darling, the one man in the world she'd ever loved enough to give herself to.

'Why are you staring at me like that?' pouted Perigenia, sensing the nurse's complete distraction, and feeling neglected. Jane forced her wild inattention to focus once more on her patient; set down the now cold, unpleasant emetic on the table without offering the actress any more; helped her into bed, tucked her up tightly, and hurried away to be alone with her tumultuous thoughts.

From below, the hubbub of a disinherited family gathering came swelling up the stairs; in the dining-room, the proud author of this turmoil sat demurely by the fire, watching everybody's baffled bewilderment. Matthew Goffe grinned at her side, sensing her enjoyment of the uproar she'd caused; and once more it was left to Sir Bennet to try to create harmony among her many victims.

'Well now, Mrs Keepdown, er, ladies and gentlemen, there is a great deal to be discussed, I feel sure. But many of those here tonight have made long and inconvenient journeys to attend this, er, h'errum, occasion. Suppose we address ourselves to the excellent spread before us?'

They had all been too preoccupied to observe the light supper which lay waiting for them; but Seely's reminder woke everyone up, and expressions grew more cheerful.

'*Let good digestion wait on appetite*,' said Matthew, 'and a jolly good idea, too!'

'*And health on both*,' came a sombre voice from the far end of the room. 'Do you not realize that it is unlucky to quote from *Macbeth*?' William Visor stared balefully about him. 'If something unpleasant should occur this weekend, you need not be altogether surprised.'

'Good gracious!' Pickbone was startled from his anxious silence. 'Superstitious—and you a solicitor?'

'It is very bad luck to quote from *Macbeth*,' repeated Mr Visor, and said no more. But the guests couldn't help pondering their virtual prisoner status in this lonely house in the arm of the river, where they must stay till Monday . . . Cicely shivered; her sister dismissed her fright as folly.

'What nonsense! Actors must be quoting it all the time, and nothing ever happens to them, does it?' But—did the lady protest too much, perhaps?

There was a momentary, bleak hush in the room. 'Ha! An angel passing,' cried Kate. 'Let's hope it was a good one, for me and my birthday . . . Now, let's all have something to eat. You'll fetch me something tasty, won't you, Martin?'

Mr Goffe shook his head in reproach. 'Matthew,' he said. 'As I think you know perfectly well, Comrade Keepdown!'

She clapped her hands with pleasure, and everyone looked towards her, expecting some fresh announcement. 'Oh, I *do* like your friend, young Henry,' she chuckled to Mr Pimpernell. 'Isn't it lucky he came with you?'

And the thought flashed across more than one mind—*lucky for whom?* Might the jaunty Mr Goffe ingratiate himself even further—to become Kate's legatee? Hadn't she kept saying that they were none of them her close relations? It was an intriguing prospect . . . and worrying.

But, as people feed, so shall they be comforted. Supper was delicious, for, witch though she might be, Alice was an excellent cook. Matthew's discovery of a tureen of tasty soup by the fire set conversation almost sparkling; everyone relaxed, and started trying to think of all that had been said before as one of wayward Aunt Kate's eccentric jokes.

Visor was kicking himself for his slip. Had Jane been there, she would have recognized his strictures upon *Macbeth*, for it had been the influence of her mother, his mistress (he shuddered), a minor actress who left the stage when their child was born, which had confirmed such a superstition in him. And, maybe, recognizing her mother's views, she might by some ill luck have recognized her father: which she must never do, must never know. He was prepared to do anything to prevent her learning the truth . . .

Matthew was able to divide his attention between Kate, himself, and the table; for he saw with amusement that Henry had turned to Cicely for help in various manœuvres which, thought a grinning Mr Goffe, hadn't been nearly so troublesome to the besplinted Mr Pimpernell in his own home. *And about time too!* opined Matthew. Kate followed his gaze, and smiled speculatively; she mused on matrimony and its strange ways, and resolved that (if it would annoy Marian to lose Cicely's home comforts) she wouldn't mind helping love's young dream along a little.

Marian herself, grimly noting Cicely's preference for the rather colourless young cousin who'd already been honoured by a private meeting with their aunt, couldn't decide whether guile or innocent friendliness prompted her to help him. Marian's lip curled as she concluded that it must be sheer good nature: poor Cicely wasn't a practical person . . . Then a low voice accosted her in a very practical way:

'The old woman's mad, of course,' muttered Gilbert, who'd materialized at her side upon noticing her calculating look. A possibly ally . . . 'I've always heard there was something funny about the family, and nobody ever talked about her side of it—well, now we know. It must have been someone clapped into the bin, and she's inherited it—what else could explain this crazy bee in her bonnet?'

'Have the goodness to remember,' a glacial Marian said, 'that *I* am related to her, by a proper blood tie—and I am quite unaware of any insanity among my relations. Though of course the shock of her accident might have turned her brain . . . she's almost ninety, after all . . . if anyone should be willing to certify that she isn't responsible for her actions —not that doctor, but an expert—'

'—maybe a judge would appoint a couple of trustees for the proper managing of her affairs,' Gilbert grinned.

'Trustees,' murmured Marian. 'Yes—I wonder . . .'

'Could be! And I expect the eldest relatives would be considered the most suitable candidates, wouldn't you?'

Marian bridled at being reminded of her age, but knew he spoke sense. 'Although her blood relations would have much the stronger claim, no doubt it could be argued that you've at least a moral claim—to a *share* in the estate . . .'

'If Uncle Luke had only left a Will, none of this would be necessary,' he whispered. They both looked across to where Kate held court, a plump, laughing spider centred in the web of destiny she'd deliberately woven, spinning the threads, choosing the flesh and blood flies to entangle in its toils. But flesh and blood can only stand so much . . .

'Now that you've agreed I have a claim, Marian, what size shareout were you thinking of?'

'I hadn't gone quite so far—'

'I think I might have a good claim to—half of it,' he interrupted smoothly, smiling at her gasp of horror. 'Henry doesn't have a leg to stand on, being only a great-nephew —I can't think why he bothered to come. But in *my* case— in yours too, of course, dear Marian—things are different.'

He gave her his famous slow, dark smile, and in one fatal moment of fascination overthrew any loyalty she had towards Cicely: avarice filled her heart: she spoke with eagerness. 'We ought not to talk like this—she'll notice us.'

'We'll meet in private, after breakfast tomorrow,' came

the pleased response. Now he had her where he wanted her! She'd agree to pressure to have the old girl certified; he might get at least a third—maybe half: the more the merrier was his candid opinion. Perigenia and her kind had cost him dear in the past for the pleasure they brought: was it really all worth the forged cheques, the scrounged cash, the borrowed apartments, the begged meals? He was growing weary, and bored. Marian (and, through her, Aunt Kate) had to be, *must* be, the answer to his problem!

With Cicely sitting beside him in a comfortable, dreamy glow, Henry had the chance to go over in his mind the talk he'd had with Kate on his arrival. He'd had to hide a grin as he saw her playing at weak and tremulous old age, propped up in bed with pillows at her back and a thick, fluffy wool shawl about her hunched shoulders.

'Come and kiss your poor old aunt,' quavered his perfectly well old aunt, and Henry saluted her rose-water cheek with care. 'If you sit beside me, I'll be able to hear you.' A shaking hand was waved towards the hard cane chair cluttered by a glass of water, a bottle of pills, a small alarm clock, and a silver handbell. Her eyes gleamed as he perched on the edge of the uncomfortable, prickly seat.

'So you've come all this way with your arm in plaster— just to see me on my birthday. I call that very sensible of you, Henry—your uncle never thought much of the brains on your side of the family—if he hadn't had me, I dare say he'd have left his money to the Cats' Home just the way I might! But wouldn't he be surprised if he walked in now?'

'I suppose he would,' agreed Henry; then, more daring: 'The two sides of the family have never got on as well as they might have done—I expect he'd be pleased that we were all here to celebrate together.'

'You're not all here together yet!' she flashed, then remembered she was a frail invalid, and sighed. 'You're a good boy, Henry, thoughtful—like young Cicely, she's not such a bad child at all, you know. Not like her sister, or that black sheep Gilbert—did you know they were coming?'

'I'd gathered something of the sort, yes.' She must have known quite well that he knew—but, if it amused her . . .

'Everyone's going to come, all my dear relations, coming to celebrate my birthday with me. Won't it be grand for such a lonely old woman, in this huge house with nothing but my own land for miles around and nobody to talk to except the servants—won't it be grand, young Henry?'

'I hope you have a marvellous birthday, Aunt Kate.' And Henry wondered why she was making such a point of reminding him how likely she was to leave a valuable inheritance—to twist a teasing knife in the wound, probably.

The evening's announcement hadn't startled him, therefore, as much as it had the others; yet, although forewarned that she was up to something, he couldn't really credit that she meant to do what Sir Bennet had sheepishly explained to them. Surely something else (even more mischievous) must be lurking behind her bright-eyed smile, her chuckling chatter, her so very gracious hostess manner . . .

'Has everyone had enough to eat? Ring the bell, Matthew, and Susan shall bring coffee—but I shan't take any, I'm tired. I'll go up to my room—Susan must tell Nurse that I'm ready . . .' As she struggled to her feet, she waved away all offers of help. 'I can manage, thank you, I'm not such a helpless old fool as people think, you know!' She leaned on her swagger-stick to address them once more. 'I'll have breakfast in my room, so you can all please yourselves what time you come down—but I expect to see everyone at lunch, Judges too—and we'll have tea all together, and dinner . . .' Her deep dark eyes crinkled with laughter at their shocked realization that she intended to go ahead with her wild plan. 'We'll spend the whole of tomorrow getting to know one another properly—won't that be interesting?'

She could certainly hold an audience. She moved towards the door slowly, but so imperiously that nobody ventured to offer assistance, though she stumbled once or twice, still gripping her stick for support. On the threshold, she spoke.

'Now I'll wish you all good night. You three—gentlemen

can find your own way out, I know, if Hour and the rest are too busy—and we'll see each other again tomorrow. I know you're all looking forward to it as much as I am!' Light footsteps pattered down the stairs. 'Here comes Nurse, to help me to bed—I need my rest, don't I? And—don't anyone forget my birthday presents tomorrow!'

She was gone. They heard her voice raised against the nurse's quiet ministrations, and the creak of the steps as the old lady heaved herself up on the banister rail. There came a distant slam from her bedroom door: and the rest was silence.

There had been murmured responses to her wicked wishes for pleasant slumbers, but little general conversation, now that she'd left them: a few hasty cups of coffee were drunk, spoons rattled in saucers, and it became clear that the party, such as it had been, was over. The old lady had certainly won this first round.

CHAPTER 7

The three Judges said their most cordial and relaxed farewells to Matthew, for they hoped that Kate had merely teased when she showed her partiality for him and that, should they encounter him at any future time long after the unorthodox weekend's proceedings, they'd be able to look him, unembarrassed, straight in the eye. It couldn't possibly be as safe as that, they knew, with any of the others . . .

Gilbert recalled his responsibilities towards Perigenia, and hurried from the room; closely followed by Marian, who wanted some time to herself before Cicely decided to come to bed. But her sister showed little sign of hurrying: Henry was too much of an attraction, and they were getting along famously together.

Matthew was pleased, but sleepy: after all, Henry hadn't driven a car through that filthy weather. 'Can you manage all the unbuttoning for yourself, or will you need me to pop along for a few minutes? Only I'm a bit tired.'

Henry was contrite; and welcomed the chance for privacy. 'Oh, don't bother, thanks—I'll be all right. It's doing things up that comes harder, because you have to hold something steady with one hand while you jiggle the button (or whatever it is) with the other.'

'It must be very inconvenient,' sympathized Cicely, 'but worse for a woman, I suppose, with all the housework— putting your hands in water, and chopping things up all the time. I expect you open tins, do you, and use the local laundry?' Quiet Cicely was pleased at her own cunning.

'We housekeep for ourselves—properly, too!' protested Matthew. 'None of this society-imposed sexual role-play for us—we revolutionaries must be self-sufficient!' Then he noticed the expressions on their faces. Did Cicely want to mother a helpless male, and did Henry want to be mothered? Quickly, Mr Goffe made amends.

'Mind you, a woman's touch about the place wouldn't hurt at all—Henry never brings home anyone who's capable of a decent pudding or cake—never brings anyone home at all, in fact. We're totally deprived of the little comforts most people take for granted,' and he sighed artistically.

'Why don't *you* bring someone home who can cook a proper cake, then?' inquired Cicely, emboldened by Henry's smile to ask personal questions of this virtual stranger.

'Oh, when the right one comes along I'll do something —but I'm not like old Henry, I'd rather play the field than settle down respectably.'

'What rot you talk!' Henry hated being described as old. 'Poor Cicely must think there's a steady stream of girls coming to the house just to satisfy your animal cravings— and it's not like that at all. We lead a quiet, tidy, respectable bachelor life—both of us.'

'Quiet, tidy, respectable, and *lonely*,' replied Mr Goffe, with a speaking look at Cicely. 'Lonely and cakeless—do you remember your chocolate sponge?'

Both young men chuckled, and Cicely smiled: 'Problems?'

'Problems,' they chorused, and Henry elaborated: 'It was during last winter's cold spell, and I swear I followed the instructions—but *something* certainly happened! Not even the birds would touch the thing, so we left it outside till the thaw, and gave it honourable burial in the dustbin!'

'What a waste,' Cicely gently reproached them. 'Give me a ring, next time, before you start, and I'll give you step-by-step instructions as you go . . .'

'We'll take you up on that,' promised Henry at once.

'But,' interposed Matthew, resolved to end the evening on this convenient high note, 'talking of *taking up*, isn't it time we all made tracks for bed? If that poor serf Susan's still about, she'll be wanting to tidy things away . . .'

Only the creaking of the boards disturbed the quiet house as the three crept upstairs. Henry murmured a warm good night to Cicely, who was encouraged to wish him good luck with his sling, and the plaster.

'He can always holler for help if he needs it,' Matthew told her, his eyes sparkling. 'And I bet he'd rather have your help than mine, any day!'

Cicely blushed, and Henry looked cross. Matthew assured them he was only joking, and they were both in so buoyant a mood that they'd have forgiven him far worse on the spot. Further farewells were uttered in muted accents, and then three bedroom doors were closed, and the house was still.

When Gilbert looked in on Perigenia, she'd tossed covers and pillows to the floor in her fitful slumber, and now lay shivering, moaning quietly. He was trying to re-establish some order about her when a creak of the floorboards made him turn. In the light from the corridor, silhouetted in a uniform, he saw a tall, slim figure, and sighed gratefully.

'Oh, Nurse,' be began. 'I've only looked in to see how, er, my friend here is doing . . .'

'She should be all right, I think,' came a low murmur, as the uniformed figure glided past him to the far side of the bed. She bent to tuck in the blankets, then looked up, and the light from the door fell across her face.

Gilbert's sharp ejaculation brought her quickly standing. 'Hush, you'll disturb her,' she admonished, surprised at her own calmness when she was sure that the pounding of her heart must wake the sleeper between them. 'She should be left to sleep . . . alone,' she emphasized.

'I can hardly believe it's you,' he muttered, seizing her arm as she passed him once more. 'I heard them speak of a nurse, but I had no idea it was you!'

'Why should you? You let me leave your life completely a long time ago, didn't you? Did you ever—think of me— the way I've often thought of you?'

'I always thought you'd grow into a beautiful woman,' he told her, still not releasing her—not that she wished it. 'And you're more beautiful than I ever dreamed . . .'

Jane was helpless beneath his animal spell, as she'd been afraid, hoping, certain would happen; she breathed a faint 'Hush!' of warning, but now her thoughts, like his, were far from that sleeping figure on the bed.

Or—*was* Perigenia sleeping? Their talk had penetrated her slumbers, which were not as sound as Jane could hope —for, having seen to Kate, the nurse had returned to the actress and given her a sleeping-draught, in her excitement quite forgetting that an overdose doesn't always work. A suicide is often surprised to vomit away all hope of an easy release; individuals with a high tolerance require a stiffer dose than ordinary people. And Perigenia was far from being an ordinary person . . .

'I must talk to you,' she heard Gilbert say hoarsely, as he raised his head from a brief but exciting kiss: he felt Jane's body trembling as his own lusts surged within him. Perigenia was out of his reach tonight, forgotten; but Jane was available, and willing. In his impatience, he pulled her towards the door, not bothering to check if anyone in the corridor might see them; and not noticing that, from the bed, his abandoned paramour observed all that happened.

Too drug-drowsy to move, the slighted actress found her thoughts beginning to clear—thoughts of rage, jealousy and hate. Now she knew why Gilbert hadn't wanted her to come with him: he'd planned an assignation with his former mistress! Flaunt as she might her own wide variety of sexual entanglements, she refused anyone else the same licence once she'd chosen them to partner her—for as long as she wished, no longer, no less. *She* was the one who ran relationships and decided when they were over: how dare Gilbert flout her this way, with that prim nurse, of all unlikely people! She must pay them both back—especially him—she'd tell that puritan old aunt everything about his amorous adventures, and shock her into disinheriting him.

As Perigenia lay in bed and quivered with hate, Jane lay quivering in Gilbert's bed under some far different emotion. She'd made no protest when he disrobed her with febrile hands, pulled her over to his bed, and jumped on her—for nothing had changed, she was still completely his, and gave herself gladly to him without inhibition or denial, rediscovering those giddy, terrifying pleasures that only he had ever shown her. When they were both sated, he'd pulled the crumpled counterpane up over them and, clasped lovingly in her arms, had fallen into a deep sleep.

Common sense returned at last, and she knew she must leave him—but not for so long! Never again for so long— never! This time, more wise in the ways of the world, she wouldn't let herself be caught, trapping him by her foolish mistake: she'd arrange something which (her remaining shreds of honesty forced her to admit) would bind him to her more strongly than ever mere sex could do.

'That was a wonderful welcome, Jane darling,' he moaned appreciatively, as she knelt in the fireglow to gather her scattered clothing. Her long blonde hair tumbled over her shoulders, and she pushed it back from her face with the old, sense-stirring gesture he remembered. 'How I wish it hadn't happened! I missed you, you know—there was never another like you, Jane—nobody could ever take your place.'

'You always liked blondes, didn't you?' She was suddenly calm, able to smile at her likeness to Perigenia, now that she could offer him what she knew he really wanted. What did it matter, what did anything matter, so long as she had what her heart most craved?

'Oh, forget *her*,' he dismissed the actress in a wild promise, prompted by memories of lust fulfilled. 'Now that we have found each other again, we mustn't lose each other—I wish we could have stayed together before, but . . .'

'But you couldn't afford it, could you? To be tied to a wife and family—it was too expensive.'

'Things still are expensive,' he quickly pointed out, in case she might be reading too much into his words. It was easy to show the automatic affection of the habitual roué, and Gilbert's old habits died hard. 'But—we must never lose touch with each other again,' he repeated his promise, and smiled his slow, dark smile as she came over to him to kneel by the bed, bending her head to his.

Yet tantalizingly she avoided his kiss. 'Would it still be —too expensive—if you inherited your aunt's money?'

'With what she's supposed to have made out of Keepdown Kurlers? Nothing would be too expensive for me then! But you can forget *that*, Jane darling. The old girl doesn't like me, never has—surely you've heard her refer to me as the black sheep of the family?'

She nodded. 'That's why I never knew it was you she was talking about—she never mentioned your name. But, if you *did* inherit her money—*would* you still want to marry me?'

Marriage had neither been promised nor mentioned; but he was relaxed in a warm, post-coital kindness, and spoke more rashly than he might otherwise have done. 'If I ended up with all Aunt Kate's cash, I'd marry you tomorrow! But she won't leave it to me—not unless we can have her pronounced unfit to manage her own affairs, and even then I'd only get a share, not all of it . . . And don't think that, because you're her nurse, you could talk her into it! I know her a lot better than you do—it's impossible.'

She ignored all this, her mind made up. 'So you promise? You'll marry me if you inherit everything?'

'You work the miracle, and I promise you'll be mine,' he agreed sleepily. 'Signed, sealed, delivered, before witnesses, anything you like. But you'll never manage it . . .'

And, as he drifted into sleep, he thought he heard a soft whisper: 'Remember! You've promised!' Then she was gone, leaving only memories behind.

At a grimly early hour next morning, horrible screechings burst upon the air, assailing sleepy ears and causing much complaint. Marian and Cicely woke, stared about them, then muffled their heads beneath the blankets; Perigenia tossed restlessly; Jane opened lust-tired eyes, and gave an exhausted groan. Only Kate, who recognized the racket, smiled to herself and was undisturbed: with an old lady's habit she'd already woken, and wasn't bothered by the din.

The others slumbered peacefully on, though the noise now metamorphosed into a grating, clanking series of thumps and slow, squelching bumps. Jane struggled to sleep once more, but failed; she stretched languorously, a smile lighting her face, the aching limbs and bruised white skin reminding her of the great pleasures she'd known. From the next room a bell jangled: Kate Keepdown wanted her early morning tea. In one final, irresolute moment, Jane hesitated; but, as further memories came stealing rapturously back, she sighed, shook herself out of bed, wrapped her dressing-gown about her; paused on the threshold to look at the cheerful face on the pillow; and went in, closing the door firmly behind her.

Marian too had failed to return to sleep. Her curler-spiked profile, sharp above the sheets, made Cicely feel increasingly guilty as her sister complained of (a) having to share a room with someone in the first place, and (b) being woken up, when it had taken her half the night to manage to sleep anyway, by ghastly screams. 'It sounds as if someone is being murdered out there,' snapped Marian. 'It's hardly the welcome I expected, after driving all this way.'

'I can't sleep either,' ventured Cicely, as a prelude to her leaving the room in a few minutes. She recognized that pinched, faded look and those brittle tones: one of Marian's migraines was on the way. She'd want to be left alone, in a darkened room, drinking nothing but iced water; but she'd hate to admit it any sooner than she must. 'I'll get dressed, I think,' said Cicely. 'Maybe I'll go for a walk, to investigate that funny noise.'

Marian lay stiff and straight beneath the bedclothes in a vain attempt to relax herself into good health. Today was vitally important: she had to be well enough to meet Gilbert, to conspire to have Aunt Kate's craziness officially recognized and her money (as much of it as possible) handed over. She couldn't afford to stay suffering in bed; she gritted her teeth, and began to cure herself by sheer willpower.

It was not pure chance that brought Henry into the corridor simultaneously with Cicely. The strange noise had woken him in the end (though he slept on the other side of the house), for, not having driven yesterday, he wasn't as tired as Matthew. At least, that was the excuse he gave for not finding out if his friend was also awake; his room was directly opposite his cousins': it was only sense to wait until he heard someone else moving around before he too appeared in search of suitable company—with a fifty-fifty chance that it would be highly suitable company indeed.

'Good morning, Cicely! Did that racket wake you as well?'

She smiled, and nodded. 'Once I'm awake, I'm wide awake, so I thought I'd explore, before the others get up.'

'Hadn't I better join you? It might be some wild animal in its lair, and then you'd need protection.'

'Please do.' Her eyes glowed: it was going to be a fine day, whatever the weather, she knew. 'We could creep up on the monster quietly, and ambush it before it ambushes us!'

They found that, if they kept to one side of the stairs, the boards didn't creak nearly so much. Only people already in

the dozing, tea-and-toast-and-marmalade-expectant stage
of an English weekend morning would be bothered by their
descent; everyone else would (unless that noise had woken
them) go on sleeping happily. The explorers came to the
bottom of the stairs, and headed without further word to
the front door—strangely, neither thought about outside
garments, or even a cup of tea in the kitchen.

The door had two large bolts at top and bottom, with a
massive iron lock, still holding its enormous key, in the
middle. Henry reached towards the upper bolt, and caught
his plaster on the protruding key, which fell clattering to
the floor; Cicely bent to pick it up, while Henry addressed
his attentions to the lower bolt.

From the far end of the hall, rolling-pin in hand, Alice
Shortcake emerged to confront the early risers. 'Why!' she
exclaimed when she saw them, 'if it ain't Mr Henry and
Miss Cicely—you give me quite a turn. Thought you must
be burglars, so I did, this early in the day.'

Henry apologized, and explained what they'd intended;
and Alice was horrified. 'You weren't never thinking of
going outdoors with neither hats nor coats on when it's bin
pouring with rain all night—and damp underfoot too, as
well as fog. You'll be dead of pewmonia within the week!'

Henry and Cicely smiled at each other for their mutual
thoughtless folly. How could they have forgotten the gar-
mentary requirements of October in the country? It was
Alice who rescued them from prolonged embarrassment:

'You pair come along of me for a hot cup of tea afore you
even think to set foot outside, and there's boots and coats
to borrow from the kitchen, if you've a mind. No need to
wake everyone with tramping about upstairs again, banging
doors and I don't know what—we had quite enough of it
last night, I can tell you, so if you really wants to go out
just to look at that pump, I'll save you a bit of bother.'

She sat them round the kitchen table and busied herself
at the range, heating water and rinsing the earthenware pot.
Cicely, after a puzzled pause, inquired:

'You say the noise is a pump, Mrs Shortcake? For water?'
'Well now, what other sort would there be, miss?'

'I mean,' blushed Cicely, confused, 'I didn't realize you don't have proper drains and sewers here—I didn't think it was so far out of the way.'

'Nor more it is,' replied Alice, filling the kettle from the tap. 'What's coming along now's the same proper drinking water as you gets in the town—but that pump as Stockfish was setting up this morning, that's for the cellar.'

'Do you pump water up from the cellar?' asked Henry. 'I never knew there was a well down there.'

Alice shook her head. 'Now, listen to me—this is an old house, ain't it? And, with some parts being older nor others, when it rains heavy, like yesterday, the river fills up and the ground gets all wet till it can't hold no more—so it all leaks into the cellar, and floods it. If we didn't have no pump, we could all be drowned dead in our beds!'

'I didn't know that,' said Henry. 'Of course, it used to be summer when I came to stay, so . . .'

'But why was the house built in such a low-lying area?' wondered Cicely, while Henry remarked:

'You'd think they could at least have cut drainage ditches to take away the seepage, if they wanted a house just here.'

'Now, don't that show you,' cried Alice, enjoying herself. 'You two don't know the half of it, see, because, when Swan House was first built, there weren't no river nowhere near it. My father could remember when Old Mr Keepdown had the Avon brought nearer with locks and such in a canal, so's he could experiment with his mechanicals, needing the water to turn wheels, and batteries, and other mysteries of his powerful cunning mind—and that's where your Uncle Luke got it from, being for ever able to invent things.

'It was a London gentleman with knowledge of such matters as dykes and ditches as arranged for 'em to be dug, and did argue as there really oughter be *two* pumps down in the cellar instead of the one we've got, but the master wouldn't hear of it—and over the years, the ditches filled up with weeds, and earth, even though that Stockfish does the best he can. And he keeps that pump working good so it's always ready for emergencies . . . like now.'

'Emergencies?' faltered Cicely, her eyes wide. 'Surely it hasn't rained as much as all that?'

Henry tried to sound reassuring. 'Don't worry, Cicely— if we're flooded out, I'll rescue you, broken arm or not— we'll doggy-paddle to the nearest high ground and shout for help to the neighbouring cows! But it sounds worth a visit —a nineteenth-century pump in full working order. We might even be allowed to turn the handle!'

As Cicely summoned up a doubtful smile, Alice laughed. 'Oh, my dear, you've no cause to worry about drowning yet —Stockfish only fetched it out along of the amount of rain we've bin having, but it'll work steady all the time and no bother, as the engine runs on petrol now, when they say it used to have a wheel with a pony, in the old days.'

'Let's go and see it—we want to be the first to find it, don't we?' invited Henry. Cicely at once sparkled her agreement, and Alice observed them both rather proudly.

'There's rubber boots and overcoats, and best take this umbrella too, even if it's stopped raining for now—you'll never know when it might set off again. Better go out by the kitchen door—them hinges at the front *will* squeak, no matter how much oil Susan puts on 'em . . .'

Out they went into the slowly-clearing day, the dewdrops heavy on the sodden earth. There was a sluggish breeze, and the branches dripped despondently; but nothing dampened the spirits of the intrepid explorers. As they rounded the corner of the house, they came upon Sampson Stockfish, heading (like them) towards the pump. He carried an oilcan, and a set of gigantic spanners. Henry promptly took Cicely's arm with his good one and, a poor invalid exercising in the fresh morning air, followed carefully behind him.

They knew his dislike of foolish chatter, and watched in an interested silence as he busied himself about an intricate mechanism assembled on the path near the cellar hatch: a quite unrecognizable assortment of cogs, wheels, and piping, a giant fretwork puzzle, toothed and knurled, with a thick pipe leading down into the bowels of the house. Stockfish oiled, tightened, and adjusted; then he cranked the heavy handle, and that same tortured squealing broke upon the air, followed by a gasping, groaning wheeze from the pipe-end in the as yet unflooded cellar.

Cicely shivered. 'Doesn't it sound like somebody being murdered?' she shouted to Henry above the dreadful din.

He nodded, but didn't reply; suddenly, the atmosphere around Swan House seemed oppressive and sinister, despite their being out of doors—his aunt's ghoulish assembly of her relations, her unlikely (and foolish?) inheritance plan— what a temptation it might be for someone to—

'You're shivering!' he cried to Cicely in an attempt to redirect his uncomfortable thoughts. 'You're cold—let's go back. We've seen what we wanted to see.'

Her face fell: she'd enjoyed her unexpected excursion, an early-morning adventure in which Marian hadn't shared; but perhaps Henry was now bored? It would be rude not to agree with his suggestion.

As Stockfish once more stopped the screaming pump, she said, 'It *is* rather chilly—I hadn't noticed.'

Henry could have kicked himself as he saw her expression change. 'Then what you ought to have is a good, brisk walk to get your circulation going and give you an appetite for breakfast. Suppose we explore a little further?'

And Cicely smiled with pleasure as he took her arm again, directing her towards the drive, leaving Sampson Stockfish staring after them, with a spanner in his hand.

His second onslaught upon the pump had succeeded in waking everyone who'd managed to sleep through the first, no matter how tired they might be. Even Perigenia dragged herself out of bed and tried to face the day as best she could; Gilbert, finding himself sprawled under the quilt in the same untidy pose Jane had left him in, grinned with gloating remembrance before recollecting Perigenia's presence—and the fact that he'd *got* to do something about one or other of the women with whom he'd importunately involved himself.

Marian, forcing a superhuman effort from her tortured frame, winced as a bedroom door cheerfully slammed: Matthew was awake. He thumped on Henry's wall; then, on going in to rouse his sleepy friend, was surprised to find him already dressed (how had he managed it?) and gone. Mr Goffe thought that on such a cold, grey day he wouldn't bother with fresh air: strong hot coffee was what he wanted, so probably Henry felt the same. Unwittingly tormenting poor Marian, who was determined to get up today no matter how ill she was, Matthew clapped Henry's door shut behind him, and headed for the lower regions.

At the top of the stairs he met Susan, who gave a little shriek when she saw him up and about.

'Oh, sir! I was just fetching you all up a cup of tea—Mr Henry and Miss Cicely have had theirs and gone out, Mrs Shortcake says, but there's plenty for the rest of you.'

Matthew was starting to remonstrate with her (he hated tea, and hated her servile mode of speech even more) when the outer door of Kate's room opened, and Jane emerged, very pale and with dark circles under her eyes. It was noticeable that her hands shook as much as her voice.

'Mrs Keepdown's not too well today,' she addressed Susan without elaboration, recalling their unhappy contretemps. 'It will not be until after lunch that she comes down—so tell Mrs Shortcake to prepare something light on a tray, if you'd be so good.' Then she nodded absently to Matthew and returned to her own room, without a further word.

'Well!' exclaimed Susan. 'What's up with missus today, I wonder? *And* her ladyship—' (jerking her head towards Jane's closed door)—'when it's usually as much as any of us is let do to make even a cup of tea—and now that nurse is asking us to fix her patient's precious dinner! Mrs Shortcake's never best pleased when along she comes, prying and poking and making sure the plates is hotted, and the tea's made with proper boiling water—as if it wouldn't be, in this house,' sniffed Susan loyally. 'But when she says *a* tray, then *a* tray is what she'll get, for missus—she never said nothing about one for herself, did she?'

Matthew, sensing undercurrents of intrigue, was eager to learn more: a true socialist, he wasn't averse to hobnobbing with the servants. 'Shall I take that tray for you?' he artfully inquired. 'It looks rather heavy . . .'

Susan blustered a bit, but he took it from her with a firm grip. 'I'll carry it for you while you knock on doors and deliver the tea,' he suggested. Susan found herself reiterating her thanks, and letting him help her right along the corridor —and afterwards, without noticing it, escort her back down the stairs to the kitchen, for a gossip.

Unfortunately, Alice gave him a brusque reception which put paid, for the moment, to his little scheme. He relinquished the tray, nodded his farewells, and headed for the dining-room: here, too, his welcome wasn't as wholehearted as he might have hoped, though the hesitant coolness with which Henry and Cicely greeted him didn't surprise him much. They'd returned with happy appetites from their walk, and were enjoying the hot food, and each other's company, without wanting anything, or anyone, else at all.

But they were innately courteous persons, and Matthew a friend; they soon forgave him for his innocent intrusion, and conversation became general. Henry described their discovery of the pump.

'Let's hope we don't really need it,' remarked Mr Goffe. 'It wouldn't be much fun to be cut off by floods miles away from anywhere, the way this house seems to be.'

'I've never heard of it happening before,' Henry quickly interposed, as Cicely's eyes clouded with anxiety.

'I thought you only stayed here in the summer?' a helpful Matthew said, before Henry hacked him under the table on the ankle. 'Oh!'

'I'm quite sure that Aunt Kate would have told everybody about it if Swan House had ever been flooded out,' grinned her nephew. 'There would have been letters and complaints and demands for assistance—and I don't remember any . . .'

'Besides,' Cicely tried to smile, 'Henry's going to lifesave me if we're flooded, aren't you, Henry?'

'Oh, there'll be no need for that.' Matthew had caught on now, and spoke more brightly than his first instincts permitted. 'This house has been here for years, so a few pints of water wouldn't harm it anyway—they made things to last in the old days—but, unless it simply pours down for weeks on end, or the river bursts its banks, I'd say we all ought to be perfectly safe.'

But there came no response as he finished speaking: they were both listening, as he had done. Outside, on the window-pane, heavy drops of rain were once more beginning to fall.

CHAPTER 8

Susan's stewed tea gave Marian just sufficient energy to stagger, with frequent pauses, down the stairs. She was quite unable to make the journey to the dining-room, however, hearing the dagger-strokes of conversation from inside, and repressing with difficulty an agonised shudder. She sank down upon the heavy oak settle, curling her trembling hand about the lion's carved head as if seeking that beast's fabled strength to face the day ahead.

It was there Gilbert found her as, emerging at last from his room with heavy eyes, dry mouth, and an aspect of exhausted debauchery, he made his own rather shaky way downstairs in search of sustenance. Finding somebody else who looked as grim as he felt unaccountably cheered him.

'My word, Marian, you look dreadful this morning. Aren't you feeling well? Did you sleep all right?' And he raised a quivering hand to hide his lascivious leer.

She closed her eyes in a fleeting gesture of surrender, then forced them open once more: in the presence of her ally, she must show no weakness. 'Just a touch of headache, thank you, nothing more. But you look rather off-colour yourself.' Was he having sleepless nights over their proposed conspiracy? Such frailty (on either part) would never do.

'Our revered aunt isn't over-hospitable in the matter of mattresses, is she?' he returned with inventive guile. 'If yours was half as bad as mine, no wonder you look tired!'

And, thus having avoided the truth, he pacified Marian's misgivings; they entered the dining-room together.

Cicely was amazed to see her sister. The quick eyes of family sympathy noted that Marian still suffered acutely: she clattered no plates and lifted no lids, and winced when anyone else did so. Cicely poured her a sympathetic cup of strong black coffee, and smiled with as much encouragement as she could muster. Poor Marian could make no reply, husbanding her strength against the interview with Gilbert yet to come, for which her brain must stay clear.

Mr Peck fortified himself with coffee as fearful as that medicinally supplied to Miss Hacket, and, once fully awake, attacked generous helpings of cooked foods and solid, thick-spread toast-and-marmalade. Matthew, thinking that some sly reference to Perigenia would irritate his *bête noire* as well as enlivening the now less lively table (Marian looking pale, the other two wrapped up in themselves), dared to comment on this surprising excess.

'Well, Peck, whatever can you have been up to during the night to need to replenish your protein so drastically?'

'If you've finished your breakfast,' snarled Gilbert, 'I can't see any need for you to hang about here any longer.'

Henry eagerly seized upon the suggestion. 'Yes, come on, Cicely. It's stopped raining again—we'll explore a bit more —if that's all right by you, Cousin Marian?' She set her glassy gaze towards him, and mutely gave her assent. 'Coming with us, Matthew?'

Matthew regarded this as one of the silliest things he'd heard Henry say for ages: suppose he accepted this tactful invitation! But, before he had time to decline with thanks, there came a bump at the door, and Susan entered with another tray, and gossip for those who cared to listen.

'Here you are, then—' slamming down a further supply of toast and clattering cups, which set Marian groaning again—'and plenty more where that came from. It's a pity for it to go to waste, what with her in a temper upstairs, and the other one not speaking to nobody.'

This sounded promising. 'Trouble?' inquired Matthew, as he helped himself to toast he didn't really want.

Susan's eyes gleamed. 'That nurse with a face like death, wasn't she—and now missus won't get up, muttering to herself in bed and never eating a thing, after I'd took it all up them stairs, which is what I never had no need to do previous—and that nurse not even seeing to her hot drink nor anything, the way she always did before . . . No doubt but what there's bin a quarrel, with 'em both in separate rooms, and not so much as ringing of a bell to get one to go in to see the other, as sure as eggs!'

'But why should Mrs Keepdown quarrel with her nurse?'

Gilbert could have answered Matthew with a fairly shrewd guess, but naturally didn't. Henry and Cicely preferred to make a tactful exit from the room rather than listen; Susan chattered on, regardless.

'*She ain't getting up till this afternoon*, says that nurse when I taps on her door to tidy up like I always do, when she gets missus out of bed—*and she don't want to be disturbed!* So I thinks to myself, Well, I don't know as I'd care for to believe the likes of *you* today, looking half crazy the way you are— so I taps on missus's door and she shouts, *Go away whoever you are!* But I just puts my head round in case something's wrong—and she throws a glass at me! *I told you to go away!* she shouts, *so don't you dare come here till I ring for you*—and not a word about her breakfast, what was made special, and she must've bin extra hungry with being so late. But *Nurse don't feel too good today*, she says—so no one's to bother *her*, neither.

'So here's the breakfast,' she concluded, 'which would greatly oblige if it could be eaten, as much as possible—on account of washing-up as well as waste. We don't want to have to throw it all away, and have that nurse accuse us of stealing it, or I don't know what else.'

This final hint, added to his earlier speculations, was too tempting. 'It looks delicious,' announced Matthew, with an ingratiating smile for the harassed Miss Grindstone. 'I'd be delighted to eat twice as much, if you had it!'

As he tucked in with gusto, Gilbert watched, wonderingly. What had taken place between Jane and his aunt? Poor, love-deluded girl—what harm had she done his cause by her tactless, pointless intervention? How would he ever, now, coax Kate Keepdown into viewing him with any degree of favour? But—there was always Marian, his second string. After the rash behaviour of Perigenia last night, Marian Hacket was probably his one hope of financial salvation . . .

The raucous revelations of Susan had juddered through Marian's head like a white-hot drill: only a supreme effort kept her in the dining-room, waiting for a private moment with Gilbert, longing to return to her bed and blessed, dark solitude. She could hardly bear to watch Matthew emptying his plate and draining his cup—which he soon did.

'I'll help you clear the things away,' he volunteered, absently piling crockery on Susan's tray. 'There's far too much for you . . .' And, with a gay nod to the two taciturn onlookers, he headed once more for the kitchen.

There followed a few moments of conspiratorial silence, as Gilbert looked cautiously round the room for any concealed eavesdroppers. 'This is hardly the place for our quiet talk, is it, Marian? Shall we go into the sitting-room?'

'As likely a place for interruptions as here,' came the stiff reply. Not only did she feel terrible, but—did Gilbert perhaps lack the necessary nerve to carry through whatever plot they hatched between them? Certainly, his common sense seemed to be lacking . . .

'I just thought they'd soon be back to clear away here—'

'And to clean the other downstairs rooms too. Somewhere upstairs would be better—by now they should have finished most of the bedrooms . . .' The effort to speak in some echo of her healthy, efficient, everyday self had been enormous, and now, as she shivered, her voice tailed away.

Gilbert chose to put his own malicious interpretation on this. 'Are you afraid of compromising your virtuous reputation, dear cousin?' For one wild second, he envisaged luring her to his room and there molesting her—but, no! Her veins clearly lacked that red blood, waiting to be stirred, which so many of his conquests possessed—she was a career spinster, dedicated and desiccated. 'We'll use my room, in case Cicely comes back to yours,' he suggested, taking her dumbness for assent. 'It shouldn't take long to work out what our united front is likely to be, and we can always meet up in Town later if we can't decide everything satisfactorily while we're here.'

'Very well.' She chose speech rather than movement to concur: a nod would have agonized her. Ramrod-stiff, she rose from her chair and led the way upstairs.

In Gilbert's room, as he shut the door, she saw through pain-strained eyes the plumped pillows and tidy covers of a maided chamber; the bold stripes of the counterpane began to dance a frenzied jig, and in silent protest she put up a hand to shut out the horrific sight. Gilbert, intent upon their plot, missed this display of weakness, and began talking at once.

'In my opinion, the old girl's thought better of all that farcical judgement business, and saying she's not well is a good excuse for not going ahead with it—which means, of course, that she still needs advice. You and I must persuade her to stop playing games with people, and to set up some form of trust for both sides of the family. If she refuses, well

—we've had doubts about her sanity, so it would simply confirm that we were right, that something ought to be done . . . Marian,' as he waited for agreement that did not, *could* not, come, 'what's wrong, for heaven's sake?'

He hurried over to her. She swayed, and closed her eyes in horror: he appeared as a bright flashing distortion of himself, a sight to sicken her. Her quavering hand went to her mouth, and she gasped a feeble request for water; but he could hardly hear her, as she swayed once more. Bending to listen, he caught her suddenly, as she collapsed.

At this moment, the door was flung open. Perigenia stood there, hair tousled, eyes preternaturally bright. 'Another woman! I thought I heard voices—and now, look at you! I'm surprised you have the energy, after last night!'

With a desperate moan, Marian tore herself from Gilbert's support and rushed clumsily from the room, pursued by Perigenia's screams:

'Go on, away with you, now he's finished with you—join the club, why don't you? Only don't think you mean any more to him than the one last night did!'

Gilbert's heart thumped with sledge-hammer bumps of dismay. He'd hoped that Jane's attraction for him, their amorous adventure, had remained secret—and here was Perigenia, blurting it out to the whole house! If Kate heard her . . . 'Peri, my angel, it's not what you think at all—'

'I know perfectly well what to think! I saw you both last night—I suppose you thought I was asleep, that I wouldn't mind if you cheated me with that unprintable nurse because I wouldn't know about it—well, I do! But how you can be interested in that dried-up epithet who was here just now, I'll never know—at least that expurgated nurse wasn't a candidate for the old folks' home! Ha, ha—I expect that's how you were hoping to get round your censored auntie!'

'Peri, please listen to me—'

'No, *you* listen to *me*! I've told you before not to mess with other women while you're dealing with me, because I don't like it one little bit. And I've got friends, if you remember, who won't want to see poor Perigenia upset—she's rather important to them, you see. Think what they'll say when they hear about you and your harem this weekend!'

'Will you *shut up and listen?*' Never mind who heard the argument now—he had to keep her quiet. He knew (by reputation only, for which he was thankful) of her influential *friends*, and had no wish to make their personal acquaintance. Now he must persuade her of the innocence of Marian's visit to his room—later, he could (he hoped) sweet-talk her out of her rage at the encounter with Jane . . . He tried once more to explain, having startled her (he thought) into silence.

But it was the silence of the coiling spring, the gathering strength. Suddenly, panther-swift, she lunged across the room, her hands ready to rake his face; he tried to catch her wrists, stumbled, and, tripping, fell to the floor, dragging her with him. There they rolled around in furious combat —she screaming and trying to savage him, her feet and fists awhirl; he clutching desperately, trying to subdue her. He had never seen so vehement a display of jealous fury on her part—not even the time when she shivered a vase across his skull and, felling him in a stunned heap, thinking she'd killed him, joined him (in hysterics) down on the carpet.

'I believe you may need some assistance, Mr Peck,' said a calm voice above their heads. Jane Nightwork stood with a gleaming hypodermic in her hand, her face as white as the crisp cap masking her neat, smooth hair. She knelt without another word to snatch at Perigenia's arm; the actress paused in her screeching long enough to scream a stream of hot and unrecognizable (even to a nurse) epithets, which Jane ignored. She caught again at the flailing arm, trapping it—there was a struggle, a stab, a squeal—and Jane stood up, breathing hard. She looked at Gilbert, panting heavily on top of the limpening blonde, and spoke at last.

'You should be able to continue your discussion rather more quietly now, I hope. You were disturbing my patient

—my other patient.' And she walked swiftly from the room.

So brisk and efficient did she seem in her uniform that Gilbert, following her with a wondering eye, could hardly believe she was the same sensuous creature who'd so delighted him the previous night. She was in command of the entire situation in a way he would never have imagined possible, all those years ago—how she'd changed, how she impressed him! What a real, whole, woman she now was!

The woman beneath him stirred, and sobbed. Cautiously, he eased himself from her, but he had no need: the drug worked. She was calmer—physically, at least . . .

Mentally, she was just as hostile. 'You've gone too far now—I hate you—don't think I'll forget this, beating me up and doping me—you and that bowdlerised nurse! I'll see you both sorted out properly if it's the last thing I do— your darling auntie won't have anyone to look after her when she's heard what I'm going to tell her, and *you* won't exactly be the blue-eyed boy any more, Gilbert Peck!'

She snivelled her way into mumbles, menacing but (by virtue of their inaudibility) less ominous than earlier ones. But he didn't need to hear what she said in order to fear it —he already knew. He had to persuade her to take back those threats, or his life wouldn't be worth living . . .

He set himself to soothe and flatter her, relying on the drug to let him caress her with no fear of physical rebuff: but Jane must have over-dosed her, for she completely failed to respond, closing her eyes almost in boredom. Soon, she was lolling back upon the floor, a dead weight, insensible. What she needed now was proper medical care . . .

From force of habit, Jane had eventually dressed herself in uniform, while remaining in her room to marvel that life could go on as normal about, yet without, her. Susan scurried about her duties, guests went in and out of rooms—if they only knew what she knew, behaved as she had behaved! Gilbert—her lost lover—little did he guess the effort with which she'd kept herself calm as she stood watching the coiled bodies writhe upon the floor, the man she loved and the blonde he'd brought, that other blonde who'd shared his sexual favours . . . those febrile, clasping hands—how very differently they had held *her* . . .

She was returning to her room when she heard strangled retchings from Marian's open door. Training prompted her to investigate, though her instinct was to stay hidden, in case the signs of her knowledge were clear for all to see— then, further sounds of suffering told her that she could not, by all she believed in, ignore what was happening.

Marian was crouched in anguish by the washbasin, hanging over it and moaning. Jane knew at once the pinched, pale look of migraine: her mother, too, had looked up at her from a haggard, strained face with dumbly pleading eyes. 'Oh, you poor thing! I know just what will help—wait here.'

Marian wasn't going anywhere, but nevertheless the nurse hurried: she rummaged in her room, then came back bearing a tumbler of greenish, fizzing liquid. 'You must drink this,' she said. 'Truly, it will do you good.'

'Leave me alone,' gasped Marian—but Jane was a nurse, a very good one. She coaxed and encouraged, while Marian was in no state to withstand her: Miss Hacket drank the lot, and wished briefly it had been hemlock. Whenever she had a headache like this, she wanted to die . . .

'You won't die.' Jane sounded amused: unknowingly, poor Marian had spoken her thought aloud. The green fluid was already having its effect. 'It will surprise you how much better you'll feel by this afternoon—you might even be able to get up for Mrs Keepdown's birthday tea!'

She hid a smile as she helped Marian to rise, leading her towards the bed, where she settled her in comfort, then drew the heavy curtains to shut out the dismal grey light. 'I'll let your sister know not to disturb you for a couple of hours, and I'll look in on you myself later—not that I think you ought to need me. With rest, you should be fighting fit by this evening . . . I'll pour you some wàter, and leave it here where you can reach it—you'll feel thirsty in a while, but sip it little and often—and rest, now . . .'

As she closed Marian's door gently behind her, she came face to face with Gilbert, who was looking for her.

'She's gone off into some kind of trance—and I thought you said she wouldn't go to sleep?' he complained.

'I said she ought to quieten down,' Jane corrected him. 'But are you sure she's not pretending for some reason?'

He led the way back to his room, and even under these circumstances Jane felt a strange thrill as she entered. Perigenia lay sprawled on the hearthrug, her eyes closed, her breathing deep and regular. The nurse felt her pulse, lifting an eyelid to check for signs of life.

'She must have already doped herself up this morning, and I ought to have thought of it,' Jane reproached herself. 'I don't know how long it will be now before she comes round—it all depends on what she took, and how much of it.'

'What she took—you mean, she takes drugs? But—I had no idea . . . Will she be all right now?'

She regarded him with scant surprise. Many people might suppose that he should have known of his mistress's doping habit, but Jane knew her Gilbert. Always one to shut his eyes to anything unpleasant, hoping that it would go away if he ignored it—a man to take the easy way out, if ever such a way could be found. 'How long have you known her?' was all she asked, in a level, unreproachful voice.

'Not long—a few weeks. And I hardly know her, really —except that she, er, makes movies—and has some . . . some rather shady friends.'

'Not the sort of lifestyle you'd want to be permanent,' remarked Jane, rising to her feet.

He shrugged, trying to be careless. 'Oh, when Aunt Kate leaves me her millions, I'll chuck it all up—I promised, remember? But—some hopes, Jane dear. She never will.'

That final word decided her. 'Your aunt has made her Will,' she told him bluntly, after checking that the door was shut. 'I witnessed it, with Sampson Stockfish—she's left all her money to you, my darling. Truly, I swear it! You're going to inherit everything.'

He stared at her in disbelief; yet her sincerity shone in her every word. 'How did you work that miracle? The old girl can't stand me—yet she's left me her money? You're the most wonderful girl in the world!' Then his face clouded with doubt. 'I can't believe it's true—Jane, are you absolutely sure?' She nodded dumbly, her loving eyes bright, and flung her arms about him. 'Then you've made history,' he murmured into her neck, holding her close in marvelling gratitude. 'If you've managed to influence her that much— my dear, disapproving auntie . . .'

'I swear she's left you everything, Gilbert—so we can be married soon, can't we? I mean—' as she felt him tense within her adoring embrace—'now you know you have expectations, we could live quite easily, couldn't we? Gilbert?'

He withdrew himself from her arms, looking glum. 'She's likely to live to a hundred,' he pointed out, 'and in any case, she's quite capable of changing her mind . . .'

As he considered the likelihood, and the problem of Perigenia, Jane considered the other three Wills, and how to prevent Kate changing her mind, and how to rid Gilbert of Perigenia permanently. And the same simple thought, different in accent and intonation but identical in fervour, came to both of them: *if she were only out of the way for good, everything would be quite all right.*

Their eyes met, and they sighed: their minds were made up. Now, there could be no turning back . . .

'She ought to be in bed,' said Jane at last, looking down upon the unconscious Perigenia. She motioned to Gilbert to help her, and between them they carried the actress to her room, where once again she was arranged comfortably beneath the counterpane. It would never do, thought Jane the nurse, to have this patient, chance-met rival though she might be, dying of pneumonia or hypothermia—or would it? But training would never let her neglect the drugged unfortunate, so she settled things carefully about the room before saying:

'This time, I can't begin to guess when she'll wake, nor

do I know how much she'll remember of what's happened
—including your rather interesting conversation just before
I appeared on the scene. It wasn't exactly restrained, was
it? Other people might have heard parts of it, too.'

'I'd better go in to Aunt Kate, and try to soft-soap her a
little. Would it be all right if—'

'I told you, there's no need to worry! Please believe me
—you might ruin everything if you start interfering. I don't
think Mrs Keepdown's well enough to see anyone today,
anyhow. She had a—a disturbed night . . .'

Their shared memories made them smile together. Gilbert looked into a rosy future, enriched by Kate's money
and the passionate adoration of Jane: last night had been
too overwhelming for him to remain clear-headed and appraising. As she'd *said* it was true, so it *must* be true—*no
matter what!*

And Jane felt exactly the same.

Heaven had blessed Matthew with one of the soundest
digestions for miles, and he was happily drinking tea in the
kitchen, absorbing as much gossip about Kate, her family,
and her guests, as his ears could take. Believing Henry to
be the likely heir, Kate's servants thought it well to ingratiate
themselves even with his friend, who might put in a word
for them when the time came: Hour and his sister were long
past the normal retirement age, and the idea of being
pensioned off into obscurity was popular with neither twin.
Praise of Henry was accompanied by a discussion of the
Great Cataract Row, and the Hackets' chances of inheriting
were dismissed with almost as much emphasis as Gilbert's.

'Nightclubs and gambling and bringing his fancy piece
to this very house—with missus so godfearing as she is, too!
And more besides,' said Alice grimly. 'Doors opening and
shutting all night, and footsteps, and wanton scurryings of
sin—all in *his room*, weren't they? And who were they from?
From madam my lady, that nurse!'

'Oh, Mrs Shortcake, are you sure?' gasped a gleeful Susan.

'What! Me what's lived in this house far longer nor you, my girl, and knowing every creak of the floorboards, and the rattle of every doorhandle—of course I'm sure!'

This absorbing topic led to a general dissection of the nurse, her character, and her relations with the rest of the staff (hostile to a man, decided Matthew). Some instinct for privacy made them withold details of those hostilities, and he tried to learn more without, he thought, showing one sign of doubt: but something must have betrayed him, for he became conscious of a sudden chill in the air.

He thanked them for the tea and the chat, complained that congenial company was too scarce out in the country, and was hanging around in the hall, wondering what to do next, when he heard a bell ringing upstairs. A breathless Susan Grindstone rushed past to answer it . . .

'Everything all right, Susan?' he inquired, as she trotted down the stairs again, looking puzzled.

'It's missus—she don't want everyone to come round for lunch today, so will I get Mr Hour to ring and tell 'em all so. Something's wrong, right enough—set her heart on it, so she had, and now, they're nobody to come till this evening, nor she don't want her cake yet, neither . . .'

She's thought better of her daft scheme, but isn't quite sure how to admit it, mused Matthew, as Susan disappeared into the kitchen. And what would the others make of it all—the three Judges, the four heirs?

Just then, the door opened, and two heirs came in, damp and breathless, yet more cheerful than might be expected of people in a non-centrally-heated, liable-to-flood country-house party during a wet autumn weekend. But the cheerful persons entering were (of course) Henry and Cicely . . .

'Only a porpoise could feel at home out there,' they told him, as he voiced his intention of going outside; so he made up his mind to play gooseberry instead, and related a choice item of news to compensate (he hoped) for his presence.

'Cancelled the lunch, has she?' remarked Henry calmly.

'I knew it would all be too much for her!' said Cicely.

'But it seems she's quarrelled with the nurse, too,' said Matthew, 'which isn't very sensible of her, is it?'

'Nobody could ever call Aunt Kate *sensible*,' grinned that remarkable old character's great-nephew. '*Cussed*, yes . . . '

Cicely giggled delightedly. 'But isn't she a marvel, for her age?' she said with some family pride—and far fewer qualms, now, about herself reaching such an advanced age alone, and unwanted: her smile was radiant with hope.

'Let's go into the sitting-room,' suggested Matthew, 'to find a pack of cards or something—a set of Monopoly might be rather suitable, under the circumstances!'

Or Cluedo. For he recalled the heated atmosphere in the kitchen, the tensions around the house—tensions of which the other two were happily oblivious . . .

But, as they agreed to his suggestion and chattered their way along the hall, the kitchen door opened with an ominous creak. Humphrey Hour appeared, walking flatfooted to the telephone, a list of names and numbers in his hand.

He was going to cancel the Judges' luncheon-party, just as Kate Keepdown had instructed: although nobody seemed to have any idea why.

CHAPTER 9

Lunch was as merry a meal as could be expected, given that the domestic staff, incited thereto by Alice, were unaccountably in a peevish mood, and half the house-guests were absent—Marian cosseting her migraine, Perigenia sleeping off her cocktail of drugs. With the judges' absence, only Matthew, Henry, Cicely and Gilbert sat round the mahogany table in the dining-room; and general conversation was strained.

Even Matthew's spirit quailed at the thought of a second day to be spent in the same company, enlarged or not: despite everyone's attempts to be sociable and easy, there was still the underlying, unspoken threat of their hostess—invisible, nursing (like Achilles) her anger. What was Kate Keepdown planning—and how would it affect them?

After lunch, it rained again, heavily. Gilbert refused to join the other three in the sitting-room, where Henry had discovered a pack of cards and a cribbage-board; instead, he fell to prowling about the house, wanting to see Marian and, because of her sufferings, prevented. Away from Jane's loving reassurances, his nerve had failed him again; he needed to re-ally himself with Miss Hacket on the belt-and-braces principle, as soon as he could. Frustration and exhaustion having taken their toll, he cast himself upon his bed in despair, and fell fast asleep.

Detective-Superintendent Lees was having a far more interesting afternoon. One look at the weather had been enough—no stroll round the garden, no sightseeing for *him*, thank you. 'Tell me some more about the crazy people in your village,' he urged. Was it precognition which prompted him?

Having last night related all she'd heard of Kate and her family history, Aunt Ellen now spread herself to include the Seely side of Bardleton life. 'You won't care if it's libel or slander, when you're off duty,' she said, simply bursting with scandal, 'but they *do* say that . . .'

That Sir Bennet Seely, last in a line of empire-builders, had been intended to make his name (as had his forefathers) in some far-flung (to begin with) outpost, followed, in due course, by a city, an embassy, and public recognition. But his early return from the colonies had been, rumour had it, part of a hasty cover-up, shielding him from the consequences of having almost beaten to death some hapless native woman who'd failed to please him.

'A terrible temper, they say he's got—though you'd never think it, to look at him . . .'

His elder sister, to whom he'd been devoted, had been the one person who could restrain his occasional outbursts with no more, sometimes, than a quelling look. Her Looks were notorious—and off-putting, betokening too much strength of will for most of the local gentry to risk their life's happiness in matrimonial undertakings. In the end, it had been the younger son of the upstart Keepdowns ('Trade, they said, inventing the Keepdown Kurler and other things') who braved Miss Seely's forceful disposition and was inveigled into a betrothal—a brief betrothal, since Lucian Keepdown eloped with his equally forceful (but prettier) Kate a few weeks before the wedding, thus ruining his family's hopes of marrying into the County.

Rather than risk heart, hope and nerves again, Miss Seely stayed to care for her brother on his return from abroad. Like her, he never married; but recently, she'd succumbed to a devastating and incurable disease, and now the baronet lived alone, except for servants, of course.

'I shouldn't think there's much love lost between Seely and Mrs Keepdown, surely?' remarked Lees, helping himself to a slice of seed-cake, and nodding his thanks when his aunt filled his teacup. 'But is it true that she's invited him, of all people, to help celebrate her birthday? A peculiar lot, your Bardleton crowd . . .'

Yet even now, he didn't realize just how peculiar, nor how closely he was to become involved with them all.

There was no seed-cake at Swan House, but Cicely, Henry and Matthew managed well enough with what Susan, meaningfully sniffing, brought in on a trolley—no birthday cake, of course, but sufficient to stave off hunger pangs until that famous Birthday Supper. Kate had sent another message via Susan: tonight, she would finally announce her plans for the ultimate disposal of her inheritance.

'Then she *has* thought better of making those three act as Judges,' deduced Matthew. 'I guessed she would!'

'They'll be able to enjoy the meal without having to feel embarrassed,' agreed Henry, and riffled the cards again. 'My deal, isn't it?'

Gilbert appeared as Cicely was making faint pre-prandial dressing-up noises. 'Aunt Kate's still hibernating, so it seems, but your sister's awake,' he announced, sneering at the signs of dissipation before him in the dog-eared playing cards, the broken matchsticks. 'And you're not to go up yet, if you don't mind waiting, she says.'

Cicely was astonished. 'Good gracious! Have you managed to speak to Marian? Usually, when she's got one of her bad heads, she shuts herself away for a whole day, at least.'

'Oh, well, I gather that, er, Nurse gave her some potion which made her feel like a new woman.' Gilbert blustered as Matthew's shrewd, slightly amused gaze met his own, rather embarrassed one: yet Mr Goffe wouldn't say anything to him, not for worlds. 'And Aunt Kate also says,' repeated Gilbert (who, in default of Perigenia, Marian and Jane, had resorted to keeping in his flirtatious hand with Susan Grindstone), 'she'll definitely be getting up for dinner, but we're not to bother dressing. And, if I may say so, my dear Cicely—you at least have no need. You look charming.'

Cicely was disappointed, since she'd looked forward to showing herself in her finery to Henry. Her admirer spoke up at once on her behalf.

'Certainly she looks charming, but I'm sure it's not what you'd planned to wear for the party, is it? Why not ignore what everyone else says, and dress up if you want to?'

Cicely smiled, and nodded gratefully, while Matthew hid a grin of amazement. What strange things the opposite sex did to people! Here was Henry, normally as polite as they come, answering back someone who (no matter what his personal opinion of the man might be) had been a guest in Mr Pimpernell's own home, and was a blood relation, too.

But the frictions currently abroad in Swan House needed, Mr Goffe knew well, absolutely no encouragement. Himself and Gilbert; Henry and Gilbert (now); Marian and Cicely (if the one too soon invaded the recuperative privacy of the other); the servants (with everyone); Perigenia with (if the servants were correct in their slander) the nurse, and (if she was the jealous sort) Gilbert Peck, probably, as well; Kate Keepdown with everyone (though that seemed nothing new). The entire weekend was turning into one of those glorious Golden Age stories where they would soon be cut off by snow and, in the middle of the night, a person unknown would come creeping into the study to stab the hostess with a dagger of obscure oriental design . . .

Since Cicely had left the room, Matthew thought he should encourage Henry to follow her example. He wanted no corpse called Pimpernell on his conscience—for if Gilbert and Henry continued sniping at each other this way . . .

'Let's go and pretty ourselves up for the party,' urged Mr Goffe, grabbing his friend by the plaster and dragging him away. 'We can't let the ladies outshine us!'

As they shut the door, they thought they heard Gilbert sigh—heavily, too. And was that thud the sound of him casting himself into a deep armchair in despair?

They were in a hurry, so they forgot him: but so, indeed, had it been. Sudden realization had come to Jane's money-hungry lover: she'd told him the truth—she *had* seen Kate sign her Will, and the old lady *had* (for whatever reason) said she was leaving all her money to him. But—had Jane actually *read* the document: could she be sure of what was in it? Gilbert knew that, where his aunt was concerned, there could be no certainty except that of uncertainty—and now, the suspense was killing him. When he could, he must talk with Marian; when he could, he must talk with Jane.

To attempt an interview by subterfuge was pointless. He was bound to be spotted either going into, or coming out of, Jane's room, where she'd insisted on staying since that last brief talk in Perigenia's bedroom. A bold strategy would be best: so he walked straight up to the nurse's door, and gave a firm, purposeful knock upon it.

'It's Gilbert Peck, Nurse Nightwork—I wonder if I could have a private word with you? A family matter which I'd like to discuss before dinner, if that's possible . . .'

Quickly she opened the door, shaking her head in reproof. 'Unless it's really important, Mr Peck, perhaps you wouldn't mind waiting for a more convenient time. I have patients to attend to,' she said in clear tones; adding, more quietly, 'You must be much more discreet, you know.'

'It won't take a minute, and it *is* rather important,' he announced, pushing her gently inside, and closing the door behind them. Then he tried to take her into his arms, but she put a warning finger to her lips and pointed to the connecting door between her room and Kate's.

'You can only stay a moment or two,' she told him, 'and I hope it really is important, or I shall be angry.'

'Surely, never with *me*, Jane darling,' he smiled.

'Oh,' she blushed, 'perhaps you're right—but, what's the trouble, then? I thought you trusted me when I said—'

'Oh, I trust *you*, all right—you've witnessed her Will, and she's left everything to me. She *said*. How can you be certain that's what the Will says? Did you read it?'

There was a noticeable hesitation on her part. 'You are to inherit everything, after her death,' the nurse told him at last. 'I promise you that—I swear it!'

A dreadful suspicion came to him—Marian's migraine, and Jane's rare medical skills—surely she would never . . .

The look in his eyes made her flush. 'Is *that* how much I have your trust?' she demanded in a bitter voice. 'My job is to heal the sick, not to . . .' She faltered. With his habitual avoidance of the acute issue, he decided to make a joke of it—let someone else take responsibility for whatever might be planned—Aunt Kate was ninety, after all!

'A jolly good idea too, if you could get away with it—ha, ha!' he leered; yet he couldn't help recalling that other death she'd had to contrive, on his behalf, all those years ago—and she'd done it, without risk to him . . .

'Seriously, my love, I've got to know,' he urged, holding her so that he could direct his powerful gaze into her eyes. 'Otherwise I'll never have a minute's peace—*did* you read the Will, as well as just signing it—or not?'

'I saw her Will: I witnessed it—and I read it. She has made you her heir,' Jane told him in a low voice, knowing now what she must do to make the half-lie the truth. His closeness to her destroyed any lingering doubts, confirmed her every resolve—she would think no more of weakening.

Her tones, forcedly unemotional, convinced him. He swept her into his arms, kissing her wildly, then released her and murmured: 'When I'm with you, I forget everything! But what about, er, my overwrought friend? Will she stay quiet for this evening—could you fix her up?'

'I can do my best,' she replied, feeling temptation surge within her. 'You don't want her rampaging through the house to tell your aunt about—last night, do you? No more do I. Though I don't think you need worry that it would make the least difference—you're going to inherit everything.'

With one swift hot kiss of gratitude he left her, saying as he opened the door, 'Thank you for setting my mind at rest. If Auntie can enjoy her birthday party in safety, then I can too—you've made me the happiest of men!' And, with an airy wave, he was gone into his own room, there to gloat over his coming good fortune as assured by Jane—the sooner, the better, but welcome whenever it should come.

Susan and Alice had helped Kate prepare for the birthday feast: Jane remained unsummoned in her room, and the pair decided silently that Kate, believing the worst of her nurse and her nephew, with her usual strictness had forbidden her the room. The thought cheered them—if Jane were now to mention the matter of missing watches, or ill-kept books, Mrs Keepdown would never take the nurse's word against theirs. And so they smiled at her vanities, chuckled dutifully at her jokes, and encouraged her to think herself the most important person in the house that day.

At the final moment before going downstairs, an unlucky, clumsy gesture from Susan sent Kate's bell clanging to the floor; in picking it up, she rang it again. From the next room came a rustle, and Jane appeared in the doorway.

'Did you ring for me, Mrs Keepdown?'

'I did not—but, since you're here, you may as well make yourself useful. Shortcake, you go downstairs to see that everything's ready for me—and you other two can get me up and about. But d'you see, Nurse, how well I can manage without you? I always told you I'd surprise everyone— haven't I surprised you? I don't suppose I'll have a nurse for much longer, do you?'

'No,' agreed Jane softly. 'No, I don't think you'll need a nurse for much longer, either.' For a moment, they gazed at each other; then Jane approached the bed and, bending, in one practised movement raised the old lady to her feet. Susan bounded forward with the swagger-stick, which Kate gripped firmly as Jane took her other arm.

'You may as well come to my party too, Nurse,' commanded Kate airily. 'I dare say you're as interested as everyone else to hear what I've got to say, aren't you?'

Jane bowed her head in silent assent, and a grin spread across the old lady's features. 'Ha!' was all she said, as the procession moved on its way; followed by, 'I hope we're having a good lot to eat tonight. I'm rather hungry, with not eating much all day—and I really intend to enjoy my birthday—I'm ninety years old today!'

A small crowd had foregathered in her honour about the dining-room table, upon which a large, decorated cake stood in state. Sir Bennet, Pickbone, and Visor, still damp from the evening's rain, were to one side; Henry, Cicely, Matthew and (slightly apart from them) Gilbert were on the other. Marian, not completely cured, sat on a chair in a corner, yet even she struggled wanly to her feet at her aunt's entrance, and joined in the chorus of greeting. Kate's glance swept over them all, and she smiled broadly.

Matthew grinned as broadly back at her, enjoying her child-like delight in her own importance, the certainty of her central position in the Swan House universe. 'May I wish you many happy returns of the day, Comrade Keepdown? And a very long life to you!'

'You're a nice young man—for a revolutionary,' twinkled Kate. 'Didn't I say so yesterday? You can help me blow out my candles, and cut my cake—' Then her eye lit upon that proud iced edifice in the centre of the table, and she said: 'Ha! No candles! I told 'em I wanted ninety, and I mean to count the lot—so where are they, then?'

Matthew, knowing he already had the entrée, offered to check at once in the kitchen. Henry and Cicely, who ought to have thought of it too, looked at each other in rueful amusement. Mr Goffe was determined that Gilbert Peck should have no chance to ingratiate himself with Kate Keepdown.

'And tell 'em to hurry up!' was her parting instruction, as he disappeared. Marian winced at her hectoring tone, but said nothing; the others remained silent.

All, that is, except Gilbert, who came lounging forward to offer his arm. 'Let me escort you to the seat of honour. Nothing but the very best for you today, my dear aunt!' And he shot a triumphant look around the room.

His ingratiating about-face almost had Marian gasping, but she restrained herself—even when he added, 'I know that *you* think you deserve the best, and I agree with you—there are no flies on you at all, are there, Aunt Kate?'

He ignored Jane's warning look: her repeated assurances had worked too well, her quiet certainty had convinced him as no passionate protestations could have done. He'd toasted his good fortune privately in the sitting-room before everyone came down; he was confident, and reckless. Miss Hacket was puzzled, fearing that he was about to abandon their plan—what lay behind his strangely-altered attitude?

There was a thump. Matthew pushed open the door: he was carrying something instantly recognizable, to domesticated Cicely, as a pastry board. It was iced, thick, firm, white; and lit by a forest of flame from the ninety candles above, trickling their melted wax of pink and blue and yellow.

'Mrs Shortcake's sorry she forgot this,' reported Matthew, wearing a singed look about the eyebrows, 'but she couldn't

abide the thought of all her decorations being ruined of by
dratted candles dripping all over them, so she made this
separately, specially for you, Comrade. Happy Birthday!'

'What a bright idea!' praised Cicely, admiring the piped
rosettes, squirls and curlicues surrounding the festive good
wishes. 'It would have been a real shame to spoil all Mrs
Shortcake's clever work with cold candle-wax.'

'And Aunt Kate will be able to cut the cake at once,
without having to fiddle around moving candles out of the
way,' remarked Henry.

Kate, who'd been suspiciously counting every candle,
gave them both an indulgent smile before returning to her
self-appointed task. The room was silent, watching her. 'Yes
—ninety, all right!' came her approving conclusion. 'So
now, everybody—just you wait!'

She took several determined puffs, and soon all that was
left of the birthday blaze was a collection of pastel stumps,
each with its soot-twisted wick feebly smoking, giving off a
tingling, acrid smell. Everyone clapped, and Kate smirked
upon them all; Matthew handed her the small saw which
lay, burnished and beribboned, beside the cake, ready to
cut it; Gilbert relieved her of the swagger-stick, and she
made a few stabbing furrows in the icing, then gasped:

'I'm an old woman, and I've done what I can—someone
else can finish it off. You, young Matthew—and everybody's
to have a piece, mind! I'll sit down for now.'

Everyone except Cicely watched the old lady as, waving
away Gilbert's arm, she headed for her chair. Cicely was
too busy suffering as she watched Matthew inexpertly cutting the cake, and crumbling its rich plumminess into ill-
hacked hunks instead of slices.

Kate's eyes never missed much. 'You think you could do
it better, don't you? Well, it's good practice for him—and
you shall hand round the slices after he's cut 'em. A piece
for everyone, mind—remember, it's for my birthday—and
so where are my presents?'

Everyone looked at everyone else; there was a scramble

for parcels, envelopes and surprise packages. Kate opened them all, clearly enjoying everything from Cicely's home-made lavender bags and the hand-made, crystallized-fruit-adorned, exclusive chocolates bought by (and shared with) Marian, to Henry's toilet-water. Kate commanded them to kiss her, and they all did—even Marian, whose effort to attend, despite evident signs of misery, brought a grudging grunt of approval from her aunt.

Gilbert provided the final flourish—a magnum of cham-pagne, to be opened immediately so that they could all drink her health. Kate regarded his slightly swaying form with a thoughtful expression, but said nothing beyond agreeing to his suggestion. 'Fetch out some glasses from that cupboard, girl,' she told Cicely, 'and, young Matthew, you open that bottle, and Master Henry can use his good arm to ring the bell. I want 'em all in from the kitchen, to drink my good health—and to hear what I've got to say, too!'

She chuckled as, hastening to do her bidding, people yet had time to look dismayed. What was she plotting? Seely, Visor and Pickbone were only thankful that she'd thought better of asking them to decide who should be her heir: but the last two wondered, for a horrible moment, if she might not be going to make revelations about them which they'd far rather keep quiet. Could she—would she? And Jane wondered, too, her heart beginning to thud—might Mrs Keepdown disappoint her, after all?

Alice and Susan, Hour and (grudgingly) even Stockfish all trooped in, and accepted their glasses from Cicely. Matthew poured, and Kate nodded; Gilbert had taken the first glass, handing it to her with a bow, and a smile. She smiled back, her dark eyes veiled, but said nothing.

'Does everyone have a glass? Are we ready?' he demanded, straightening himself up and facing the company. 'Then . . .

'Happy birthday to you,' he began, slightly slurred.

'Happy birthday to you,' chimed in Matthew, Cicely, and Henry, tunefully and with enthusiasm.

'Happy birthday, Mrs Keepdown,' the doctor, the solicitor and the baronet found themselves harmonizing.

'HAPPY BIRTHDAY TO YOU!' roared the entire room, as Kate beamed, and clapped her hands.

'Three cheers for Aunt Kate!' cried Gilbert. 'Hip, hip—' and they were loudly given. Even those who had good cause to fear, or at least dislike, the old lady sitting so plump and complacent before them, felt somehow that they must salute ninety years of an outstanding personality.

'And now,' she began, when the tumult and the shouting were done, the last crumbs of cake washed down by the dregs of the champagne, 'it's time for me to make my speech . . .' Everyone froze into silence. 'Or—should we have supper, first?' she naughtily mused. 'Yes, you know, maybe we will. Let's have something else to eat besides cake, hey?'

The kitchen staff scuttled away, reminded of their duty, accompanied by Stockfish, who was muttering darkly about the pump, and the river, and the rain. The guests now unfroze, and began to talk among themselves, waiting. Only Matthew could chat quite calmly to Kate, and was doing so, when the squeak of trolley wheels heralded Susan's return, and supper.

It was a good meal, and liberal of wine: people tried to enjoy it, and some even managed to, while others dismally failed. Gilbert was *not* one of the latter; nor was Kate, who ate and drank with relish. Neither Pickbone nor Jane ventured to scold her for over-indulgence, and it was almost as if she defied them in every way she could.

Susan came in to clear away; dishes were passed along the table, and she piled them on the trolley to take them to the kitchen. Nobody saw how it happened—but she stumbled, the wheels jammed and skidded, and, with a crash like a thousand bomb-blasted windows, over in the doorway went the lot—plates, dishes, lids, cutlery, with Susan a shocked and screeching casualty on top of them.

'You clumsy baggage!' cried Kate. 'You're fired!'

Alice rushed in, closely followed by Hour. One began to upbraid poor Susan, the other to clear the mess on the floor; Miss Grindstone went into hysterics, and Pickbone, professional and stern, slapped her soundly before telling her to get on with helping Mrs Shortcake. Kate said, 'Ha!' in a loud and meaningful manner.

'Don't fret yourself, Mrs Keepdown,' urged Jane, holding her wrist as she felt her pulse. 'Please try to keep calm—it won't do your blood-pressure any good if you don't.'

Kate sniffed, but suffered the nurse to hold her in one cool hand: a mark, so the jealous eyes of the servants soon decided, of her return to their mistress's favour. In fact, it was a combination of shock, excitement and tiredness which let her permit the liberty, but they weren't to know that, and, moodily brooding, they cleared away. And it was while they were completing the finishing touches that yet another shock befell them: Perigenia came downstairs.

The sounds of revelry from below had partly woken her, but Susan's discordant mishap had finally driven out all possibility of sleep. Still rumpled, wrapped in a silk kimono, her hair a tousled aureole about her head, with the hall light behind her, she made a striking figure.

'Good gad!' exclaimed Sir Bennet, ogling her déshabillé more openly than anyone else. 'Gad—what a woman!'

Gilbert glowered at Jane, who silently pleaded for understanding: the actress's built-in immunity had again led to a miscalculation. But what harm could she do, now?

'Oh dear, Mrs Keepdown—how sorry I am to have missed your party,' drawled Perigenia in a wicked purr, gazing on the signs of revelry accomplished. 'Gilbert, you naughty darling, you shouldn't have let me sleep so long— I'm sure you never meant me to wake up *now*, did you? But, since I'm here at last—even if it *is* at the end of everything —Mrs Keepdown, do let me join in the celebrations!'

Gilbert understood, far better than his aunt, what Perigenia had really meant. And, as he watched Kate overcoming her surprise and scruples, actually welcoming the woman

into the room, once more he wondered about her intentions
—about the intentions of them both.

'Come on, girl, you may as well make yourself at home,'
invited Kate. 'There's still some cake left, and wine—now
you, sir, Gilbert, do the honours for your . . . friend!'

'Thank you, Mrs Keepdown—*and* Gilbert—how kind!
It's such a change to meet someone who welcomes company
instead of hating it, the way some people do—I know some
very unfriendly people, don't I, Gilbert dear?' And, her
position having been made clear, she ignored him from then
on.

She now threw herself into being as partified and agree-
able as possible; and, being an actress, managed a fair
performance. She was gay, bright and amusing—she flirted
with every man in the room except Gilbert and Henry (who
was far too wrapped up with Cicely); but she never forgot
that Kate was the queen of the evening, paying her merry
compliments and teasing her, yet never overdoing it—for
she was as shrewd as Kate herself, and recognized when
enough was enough.

In fact, apart from the threat of Kate's postponed Grand
Announcement hanging over them, nearly everyone found
themselves having a surprisingly good time; but the underlying anxiety, the uncertainty, remained, and Kate seemed
to be revelling in her cruelty to the curious.

'Let's open another bottle, young Matthew,' she snapped
at a totally unexpected moment. 'Fill 'em all up—but we're
not drinking any toast this time! *This* time, it'll be for
medicinal purposes only—because, let me tell you, some of
you are going to *need* a drink!'

'Would you like us to leave the room?' asked Matthew,
as he struggled with the corkscrew. And Perigenia rose to
her feet without a murmur.

'Oh, sit down, sit down! Don't fuss—there aren't any
secrets in this house, you know!' So the actress sat; and
Matthew, having removed the cork, poured. Everyone in
the room held their breath.

'Well now—are you all listening to me?' demanded Kate Keepdown, her eyes bright, her breath coming faster as she spoke, her face flushed with excitement. 'Nobody's fallen asleep, have they? Good . . . Now then—I've made up my mind. I've thought it all over, very carefully, and I can see that I've got no real choice—so . . . unless anything happens to make me change my mind, of course—I suppose it's only right that the Keepdown money should stay in the Keepdown family, and I've already decided what to do about my Will, without any help from anyone . . .' She stared round at her enthralled audience, and Matthew could have sworn he almost saw a wink as she looked towards Jane. 'So I'm leaving all my money,' Kate concluded in triumph, 'to *you*, Gilbert Peck!' There was an audible gasp. 'And now, I'm tired, so I'm going to bed. And I want someone to give me a box of matches—and a candle as well, if you'd be so good, young Matthew.'

He rose to do her bidding, and she motioned to Jane. 'I still can't manage everything on my own, so you'd better follow me up, hadn't you?'

Then, in a stunned silence, everyone watched as she made her momentous exit, stumping her swagger-stick as she walked; and the door slammed shut on a thousand forlorn hopes.

CHAPTER 10

Nobody knew quite what to say next. Gilbert, his mind dazed with disbelief, poured himself a stiff peg of whisky to celebrate the ultimate proof of Jane's promises; Jane gave him a quick, conspiratorial smile of relief. The three Judges, in their own ways, were also relieved: mostly because Kate had, after all, made up her mind without bothering them. Now it was to be hoped that the matter was at an end. Indeed, Sir Bennet went so far as to ogle Perigenia in a very appreciative way, and seemed put out that she chose (since Kate was gone) to turn off the charm and the gaiety.

She regarded Gilbert with a calculating light in those hard emerald eyes. If he was going to get all that lovely money one day, might it possibly be worth her while to throw in her lot with him again . . . ?

Henry gave Cicely's hand a comforting squeeze. 'Oh, well, you know what she's like—she may not really mean it—or, if she does, I wouldn't put it past her to change her mind the very minute we've all left the house!'

Cicely chuckled, and nodded; Matthew grinned. Marian's voice would have frozen the blood of a salamander:

'I always said she was crazy, and this ridiculous choice proves it! After all she's said about our family's black sheep, over the years—for her to behave like this! I am sure that any *competent* mental health *specialist*—' and she directed a withering look towards Dr Pickbone—'would have to certify that she's totally unfit to make such a decision, considering the accident, and all the excitement of her birthday—and when you think of her age . . . as soon as we're back in London, I'm going straight to Harley Street.'

'Now, Miss Hacket,' Pickbone rushed into speech, 'I must advise you that I think you'd find it very hard to persuade anyone to, er, certify that your aunt's state of mind isn't sound—strong-minded she undoubtedly is, and eccentric too, but certainly *not*, er, off her head. And, with respect, I have known her far longer than you have done.'

'Really, Doctor, anyone would suppose you to have some personal axe to grind, the way you speak up for her!' Did she, he wondered, observe his guilty start—did anyone else? Luckily, Jane had just left the room. 'And, until my aunt made this—disgraceful announcement, Gilbert Peck and I were in complete agreement that she should be examined by a qualified psychiatrist. Which for my part I still believe! After all, she's *my* aunt, a blood relation—Cicely will bear me out when I say that some of our relations were very strange indeed! Obviously, that streak is now coming out in poor Aunt Kate—so the best thing for her is that she should have proper medical care.'

Cicely's eyes clouded as she looked at her sister. 'Yes, some of them were a little odd,' she confessed, 'but not mad, exactly—' (for Henry's benefit) '—just strange, that's all. Though I suppose,' she added, in sororal loyalty, 'her age, and her accident, might have made it worse . . .'

Marian glared triumphantly at Peck and Pickbone. 'You see? My sister agrees—we're going to Harley Street now!'

It was glorious, fighting talk. She glared at Gilbert—he glared at her, sensing a worthy foe, far more determined than ever she would have been as a conspirator. And she'd roused his old doubts again . . . He poured himself a drink.

Perigenia, with the pop-eyed baronet gazing gloatingly down her cleavage, still eyed her erstwhile lover with much interest. Good looks—good technique—good prospects . . . of course, there was that nurse, but . . .

Matthew finally found something to say. 'Wasn't the old devil simply bubbling over with excitement? Whoever would have thought she'd pull a stunt like this—I dare say it's even surprised *you*, eh, Peck?'

Even now, Henry wanted to avoid friction. 'You can well believe *anything* of Aunt Kate,' he said with pride. 'And besides, as things stand now—' purposefully, he acquired Cicely's hand once more—'nobody could say that my cousin here was about to marry me for my money, could they?'

Cicely blushed, her mind instantly made up. 'And nobody could say you were marrying me for *my* money, either!'

Two disappointed legatees smiled into each other's eyes. Matthew chuckled, pleased with his own small part in this affair; even Marian, rash though she considered her sister's choice to be, merely sniffed. But, for everyone except the newly-affianced pair, all pretence at a party atmosphere was over. Kate might have left the room, but her memory lingered on; those who went in fear of her revelations could bear to stay in the house no longer. Pickbone and Visor stood up, and announced that they must go, before the weather got any worse.

Sir Bennet, lecherously twittering beside Perigenia, saw himself as once more the daredevil young Benny, ladies' man, and ignored their signals of departure. They decided to leave him to it, for she was responding (in a small way) to his advances, though no one could know that it was the mere instinct of a past mistress of fascination: he might manage to impress her, they believed, and in any case it wasn't any of their business.

Nor did it exactly seem Gilbert's business to act as host in Kate's absence—yet he smoothly rose to the occasion. 'It seems a shame to break up this enjoyable evening, but I should hate to detain you against your will. You both came together, didn't you?'

They murmured their assent, followed by their goodbyes, and Mr Peck led the way through the hall with a proprietary air which maddened the departing guests. However, they took polite leave of him, shrugging on their overcoats and darting out between the raindrops with bonhomous expressions of farewell and thanks. Gilbert shut the door without waiting to watch them go, and, as they settled themselves in the car, Visor remarked grimly,

'That man is riding for a fall, I think. I agree with young Pimpernell that she is likely to change her mind.'

'Indeed she is—about some things,' replied his friend absently, struggling with the ignition. The starter motor wheezed, and the engine coughed bronchitically; Pickbone turned the keys, clicking them backwards and forwards, but still there was no spark of proper life.

'Your plugs are probably wet,' remarked Visor gloomily. 'Would it help if I tried push-starting you?'

'I certainly want to get home every bit as much as you,' replied Pickbone, although he couldn't explain this feeling, which emanated from his friend in powerful waves. 'But I'm not letting you push a thing this weight around in the mud, at your age—and, apart from the risk to your heart, what about the risk of pneumonia? *I'll* get out and push—or we could always wait until Seely comes out, and try cadging a lift from him.'

'Is he likely to appear before we freeze to death? For he looked rather—preoccupied, back in the house.'

'Woman brought along by Peck . . . I wonder, you know, what Kate really thinks about it all. If you ask me, tonight's affability was just the lull before the storm.'

'Let us hope,' said Visor fervently, 'that she does not cut him out of her damned Will and start this judging nonsense all over again. My nerves could never stand it.'

'I wouldn't put it past her, at that—she's a very tough, strong-minded old lady . . .' And Pickbone sighed, his thoughts heavy. He gave a final experimental twist to the car keys, and jabbed viciously on the accelerator—and, with a tentative groan, the engine spun slowly into life, jerking once or twice with an unpleasant grinding sound, but eventually sparking successfully on all four cylinders. Freedom from Swan House, after all!

He revved the engine again, then switched on headlights and wipers. These scraped their rubbery way over the windscreen, revealing an almost solid wall of rain falling into huge, lively puddles; wherever the drive wasn't deep in water, it was awash with mud forced up from under the gravel by the pelting drops. As Pickbone released the hand-brake and spun the wheel, spraying mud spattered out from beneath the tyres, and the car skidded as it moved.

Visor smiled grimly. '*Let the great gods, that keep this dreadful pother o'er our heads, find out their enemies now!* A pelting, pitiless storm indeed—how glad I am that I am not driving.'

Pickbone strained forward, his hands gripping the steering-wheel. 'It's murder tonight,' he said, and drove on.

Henry and Cicely still sat decorously entwined in the dining-room, looking pleased with themselves and un-worried by anything else. Marian regarded them, wistfully but with an air of discontent: surely her silly sister and her

young man must see that there were more important matters
to arrange?

Matthew followed her gaze, and nodded. 'Isn't it amazing, Miss Hacket? When old Henry goes, he certainly goes,
with a vengeance—and I'd say he's got a prize there.
Your sister seems just his type, sweet and charming and
domesticated—'

'And impractical,' she snapped in conclusion. 'Let's hope
your friend has more common sense than he appears to be
displaying at the moment—maybe you should talk to him,
to explain that it would be in all our interests to get together.
To do something about Aunt Kate, I mean . . .'

'I'm only Henry's lodger, Miss Hacket, though I hope
I'm a friend as well—but your family affairs are nothing to
do with me. I'm only involved at all because Henry broke his
arm and couldn't drive—besides,' as storm-clouds furrowed
Marian's brow, 'from what I've heard and seen of your
aunt, she's the type to enjoy a joke at the expense of others.
Like saying tomorrow that she was only fooling tonight . . .'

'Only a fool could enjoy such a joke—pretending she'll
leave all her money to Gilbert Peck, indeed!' She spoke with
scorn and volume. Mr Peck, who'd returned unobserved
from seeing-off Visor and Pickbone, heard her clearly, and
wandered over, glass in hand, his dark face sneering.

'Why, Marian, how wonderful of you to be so concerned
over our poor, dear old aunt's health! And, Goffe, how
very kind of you to interest yourself in our private family
business!' He chuckled, and drank deeply. Marian set her
teeth but said nothing; Matthew was tempted to thump
him, but set his own teeth, and ignored the provocation.

'Why so quiet?' laughed Gilbert. 'I thought, just now,
that you two had plenty to say to each other!'

'Now see here, Peck—' began Matthew; as the doorbell
rang with a booming, doomladen peal which startled everyone.

'What late and riotous hours we keep in the country!' Mr
Peck once more took the host's part. 'I'd better see who our

visitors are . . .' He bowed ironically deep to Marian, and made for the dining-room door. As he opened it, they heard Humphrey Hour shuffle past from his lair, grumbling at being disturbed so late at night.

'Sorry to bother you, Hour—er, Peck,' amended the voice of Dr Pickbone, as Gilbert arrived to interfere. 'But—we can't get through, only a lifeboat could. The Avon's burst its banks, and every road's flooded. We're quite cut off.'

Visor continued the melancholy tale. 'We must beg the hospitality of a sofa for tonight at least, I'm afraid . . .' And only Dr Pickbone could fully appreciate the sorrow with which he made that request.

Gilbert rose to the occasion. 'You both look soaked and frozen—certainly you must stay. Seely too, of course!' But his raised tones of invitation could not penetrate Sir Bennet's concentration on Perigenia's cleavage.

'It's at least knee deep in the first dip in the road you reach, coming from here,' explained Pickbone. 'I got out to check how bad it was—and Visor ended up having to help me push the car back. Another six inches, and the engine would have drowned completely.'

'So here you are, come back to be marooned in style with us,' remarked Gilbert, exuding welcoming generosity as the jellyfish exudes poisonous filaments. 'Hour—you take the coats, please—and fetch Alice and Susan, they'd better make up beds in the unused wing—'

'Excuse me, Mr Peck, but I think that would be unwise.' Jane had finished putting Kate to bed, and was coming down the stairs. 'Those rooms haven't been aired, and the sheets might well be damp—and both gentlemen are so wet to begin with! I believe that rugs and blankets in a warm room will be a great deal safer, don't you—er, Dr Pickbone?'

'A shake-down in the sitting-room, a car rug or something like that will be fine,' he agreed, unable to meet her eyes.

'Ah, Mrs Shortcake!' Gilbert greeted Alice and explained again, with a tippler's insistence, what Hour had already told her. She listened unmoved, until he concluded: 'Nurse here will help you, to make sure that the blankets aren't damp, and that everything is arranged satisfactorily.'

Her flinch was visible to everyone but Gilbert. 'You'll not find no fault with my housekeeping, Mr Peck, not nohow! I do as missus tells me—but, seeing as how this is by way of being an emergency, and the other wing ain't maybe all as it should be with not being used regular, then Susan and I will tidy out some covers from a few cupboards. There'll be no cause for Miss Nightwork here to bother herself—I'm sure she's got other things to busy herself with tonight.'

She gave them both a meaningful leer, but, while Jane saw it, Gilbert remained oblivious. 'Oh, many hands make light work, you know, Mrs Shortcake! Just go along to keep an eye on things, would you, Nurse? Our guests must be made quite snug and comfortable, mustn't they?'

Mr Peck led his storm-tossed visitors back to the dining-room without waiting to observe the protesting looks on the faces of Alice, Hour, Susan and Jane: if a man can be drunk on self-confidence, then Gilbert was intoxicated indeed. He poured Pickbone and Visor lavish tots of whisky, and topped up Sir Bennet's glass with a sideways wink of congratulation to Perigenia, who seemed still undecided whether to permit the attentions of the squiffy baronet in preference to some attempt at regaining Gilbert's particular favour. The only favour he showed her, however, was the careless slopping of quantities of whisky into her already full glass—he'd cast all caution to the winds, and was no longer in the least concerned about the future.

Jane appeared in the doorway. 'We need some help shifting the chesterfield—can anyone lend a hand?'

A chorus of *please don't bother* and volunteered help was drowned out by Gilbert's jovial, 'Delighted to assist—we must see our guests properly settled, mustn't we?'

With his exit, such conversation as there had been among the others finally faded, and there were general mutterings about preparations for bed.

'After all,' said Marian, 'we have a long journey back—

and Cicely will be reading the map again tomorrow.'

Cicely blushed, then giggled, and Henry smiled as he told her sister, 'That's only if the roads are clear, remember. After all, it's still raining out there!'

Pickbone nodded. 'Last time the Avon flooded as badly as this, it was two or three days before Swan House was in touch with the world again—you may have to resign yourselves to an enforced stay here, I'm afraid.'

'You do not number yourself among our merry throng, from what you say,' remarked Visor, unable to conceal the wistful tone of his voice.

'It wouldn't do for a doctor to be out of reach of the village, in case of emergencies—I'll phone someone to get me a rowing-boat tomorrow, and I'll borrow a car once I'm on dry land again. I could probably give *you* a lift, Visor— but if the rest of you want to leave in your own vehicles, I'd guess you've another day ahead of you before you can.'

This optimistic prediction confirmed everyone in the resolve to go to bed early, in the childlike hope that things would be all right in the morning. There was a general exodus, leaving behind only Pickbone, Visor, Seely and Perigenia; there was the sound of feet going up the otherwise silent stairs, a muted babble of good nights, and bedroom doors then opened, and shut again upon the night.

The furniture-shifting was done. Gilbert made his way, with Jane, along the hall; in the shadow of the great newel-post at the foot of the stairs they paused, to snatch a few private words before going their separate ways.

'Darling Jane, you're a marvel! I don't know how you did it—and I don't want to know, either! But the old girl's really turned up trumps for me—I mean, for *us*. Just as soon as—I come into my inheritance, everything will be as wonderful for us both as it always ought to have been!'

He should never have reminded her of those dark days of solitary shame, shouldn't have thought first of himself and only afterwards of her—just as he'd done then . . . Suddenly she couldn't bear to be less than totally honest with him.

Were they not going to be together for better, for worse—
for richer, for poorer . . . after all?

'I'm afraid it's not quite as simple as that. She's made a
Will, definitely, leaving everything to you—and it was
signed, and witnessed, just as I told you.'

'Then what's the problem?' he demanded, leaning over
her and breathing warm, loving whisky-fumes into her face.

So she told him what the problem was.

'*Three others?*' He was horrified, forgetting to keep his voice
low, and she shushed him frantically. 'But—you said earlier
that I'd inherit everything—and then tonight, *she* said . . .
and then she asked for a candle . . .'

'She said *so long as nothing made her change her mind.*' The
helpless panic in which he turned to her confirmed her
own clear-headedness, that quiet reliability which had so
appealed to him, those repressed maternal instincts which,
she knew, were the complement of their strong attraction
for each other. 'But—I can promise you, she won't change
her mind—she'll burn the other three Wills, and then—'

'Suppose the old devil burns the wrong one? Or the right
one, after all—she can go through this whole performance
every week, if she wants.'

'Unless,' she said stoutly, 'she doesn't live long. She is an
old, sick woman, remember—her heart isn't all it should
be. She's already had one spasm since I've been working
here—and, if she should die . . .'

Sober with shocked admiration, he stared into her steady
blue eyes. Was it only the shadows in the hall which made
them seem so deeply, darkly determined? 'What a wonderful, ruthless darling you are!' He tried to sound untroubled
—lighthearted . . . but he couldn't repress a shiver.

'Listen!' she breathed. 'Somebody's upstairs!'

'I can't hear anything—are you sure you did? And—do
you think they could have heard us?'

'I believe they might have been listening, but you needn't
worry. Your aunt has had time now to burn the other three
Wills, as she said she would do—'

'But now, other people know about that! If—'

'When I go in to her, I'll find out. But you mustn't—'

Then the dining-room door burst open. Out lurched Perigenia, drunken and shouting, hanging on to the heavy brass handle for support. 'You horrible, undersized little creep, how dare you suggest such a thing? No *real man* ever spoke like that to me before—and I've seen schoolboys who were more man than you! You make me laugh!' And she laughed—mocking, echoing, cruel. Then she slammed shut the door, hiccuped, and began to weave her way to the stairs.

There was a rattling wrench, and Sir Bennet stood in the doorway, shaking, his face flushed, his shrill voice still shriller with rage as he cried: 'Baggage! Wanton woman—miserable, whoring flirt! Jezebel, jade—'

Visor and Pickbone rushed to restrain him, and had to hold him back as he struggled and roared. Perigenia paused on the bottom stair to giggle at his impotent ragings.

'Poor little man—silly little Seely! Thinking he could score with *me*! I'm not some two-bit totty who's thankful for any offers she gets—I'm fussy, I am!'

'You cheap trollop, leading me on like that all night!' cried Sir Bennet, and was dragged inside by his friends. The heavy oak panels muffled his anger, and Perigenia went on her way unmolested.

'What charming, ladylike friends you have,' murmured Jane. 'And how unwise of her to provoke him—he looks like the smouldering sort, capable of bearing a grudge for years.'

Gilbert, though shaken, shrugged the episode off. 'She was only flirting, for heaven's sake—he just didn't understand the rules of this particular game. I mean, what else is there to do out here in the back of beyond?'

'I really can't imagine,' she said, flinching at this infelicitous remark. 'And now, I must see to my patient.' With that she left him; and only as she vanished at the top of the stairs, heading past Perigenia's door towards (at a guess) Kate's, did he realize how he must have angered her.

'Women,' he muttered, and returned to the dining-room.

The rumpus seemed to have died down, now that Seely had been denied further sight of his tormentor, and the three men sat discussing who should sleep where—which was difficult, since nobody had told them what the arrangements were. But it had been the first topic to come to mind, so they all were worrying away at it with fervour.

They greeted Gilbert eagerly, and he managed to explain the possible sleeping system. After discussion, Seely, the smallest and lightest, chose to take the two large armchairs pushed together in the library; Visor opted for the sitting-room chesterfield, pulled across the dying embers of the fire; while Pickbone ended up with the massive leather sofa in the opposite corner, sheltered from the draughts of the open room by a solid, tall screen.

With quiet jokes and forceful plumping of cushions, they settled themselves for the night; Gilbert tramped away up to bed; and, apart from the rhythmic thudding of the pump outside in the rain, Swan House seemed at peace.

Kate had insisted on a full explanation for all the bustle, which she claimed was keeping her awake. It was the first conversation of any length she'd had with Jane since that other, earlier in the morning, after which the old lady had seemed in such a mood; but now, her spirits were positively sprightly at the news the nurse brought.

'Cut off by floods, hey? And the house full upstairs—screeching women, I heard her, the hussy!—and downstairs, too? Three of 'em, all unexpected—and this house, cut off by floods. Well, well. Whoever would have thought it?'

For a moment, they were both still, listening to the rain falling, the pump working, and all the other noises of the night; then they began the second stage of their colloquy.

The rain still teemed down, slashing against the windows, eddied by the rising wind round and round the lonely house. The wind moaned, the pump groaned, and the snuffling mumbles of sleep turned to regular, relaxed breathing in every room in Swan House—except one.

She went slowly down the stairs, clutching the banister for support, hoping nobody would hear her; but the damp-swollen boards creaked no longer, and she reached the bottom in safety. There she paused, listening; and made her unsure way across the hall to the library, not daring to put on a light as she heard the alcohol-deadened snores of Sir Bennet. But he wasn't, she found, her goal; she shut the door as quietly as she could, and went towards the sitting-room.

When she came out, she walked unsteadily, closing the door behind her with a clumsy click; yet she was unconscious of the noise, and sank upon the carved settle to regain her strength before climbing the stairs once more. Her breath came fast, her heart fluttered; when she reached the great newel-post, she held on to it, resting her hot forehead upon it, feeling its knobbiness cold against her clammy skin.

It was the last thing she was ever to feel. The figure waiting patiently in the shadows moved forward—and struck, and struck again—quick heavy blows which led to a dull thud and a slither, as she fell to the floor. In her fall, she rolled over, and lay, curiously twisted, upon the dark woven rug at the foot of the stairs.

The murderer bent, and put a hand on her neck—no heartbeat, not even a flicker. Her feet blocked the stairs, and they were pushed on the rug. The bundle which had been a living person but a few moments before was tidied out of the way, shoved under the dark oak table where nobody would find it until, wondering at her absence from her bed, they might institute a search.

The murderer checked for bloodstains—there were none. And then, with a low laugh, the still-held weapon was laid out of sight, under the table, neatly beside her on the rug. One last look at the grimly-shadowed bundle, and then it was left alone in the cold, dark hall; while the murderer went back to those slumbers interrupted for so very violent a purpose.

CHAPTER 11

Susan Grindstone was known in Bardleton to be walking out with Police Constable Clement Perkes: it was therefore to him that she turned when she made her unpleasant discovery upon rising next morning, to give the customary swish with a broom around the floor of the hall and under the table. Her piercing shriek roused the rest of the household, and PC Perkes, once he'd understood what she'd found, was able to confirm her shocking news by speaking to Matthew Goffe. Matthew's room, being at the top of the stairs, allowed him to reach the scene of the crime before anyone else; and it amused him, revolutionary that he was, to be assisting the police with their enquiries.

Good village bobbies know all about their village, and PC Perkes was no exception. He was already acquainted with Miss Ellen Silence, and had heard on the grapevine of her visiting nephew: with all roads blocked, and reinforcements at least a frogman's length away, Detective-Superintendent Lees looked like the answer to prayer.

Lees advised Perkes that he was happy to help until the proper authorities could arrive, but that he couldn't swim. Perkes produced gumboots, and a rowing-boat.

'You win,' sighed Lees. 'Bang goes my holiday . . .'

He professed himself unable to row, and found quiet fun in counting the number of crabs which Perkes caught in their progress along the high street—along the right-hand side, as Lees, who knew his Haddock, was quick to instruct the oarsman. Away from the village, it was a slow and effortful slog, bumping over hedges and avoiding trees and haystacks, until Perkes shipped a dripping oar, and pointed.

'Over there, sir, beyond them trees, that's Swan House.'

They scrambled out of the boat on to what might, for want of a better term, be called dry land: it was a quagmire, and

Lees blessed Perkes for the boots, even though they were at least one size too small—for, standing a shade under six foot three, he had feet in proportion to his height.

'It's going to be,' remarked Lees, as they trudged thick-footed through the mud, swinging their legs in weary curves, 'an interesting morning. Just the two of us, until the rest arrive—I'm glad you managed to telephone safely, Perkes—but it'll give us a chance for some genuine detection as it used to be in the good old days, before it turned so scientific. All we'll be able to do is talk, and listen—and hope that whoever did her in will give himself away.'

'A funny lot, hereabouts,' puffed Perkes as he strove to keep up with his companion's long legs. 'I don't know if your aunt's told you anything, sir? It would save—'

'She certainly has! I know all about Mrs Keepdown's elopement with Sir Bennet Seely's sister's intended, and *his* sinister return from the Empire under a bit of a cloud, *and* how Mrs Keepdown won't make a Will even though her family's a bit untidy—oh, I've heard all I could ever want to hear, and then some!' Lees nodded towards Swan House, floating like a stone frigate among the dull brown ripples of the surrounding floods. 'I even know why Sampson Stockfish is supposed to hate all women—that *is* Sampson Stockfish over there, isn't it—by that enormous pump thing?'

'Sampson Stockfish,' confirmed Perkes, with a sigh. 'One of the most perversious and cantankersome old bodies—with no mention of Mrs Keepdown, that's to say—as I may ever hope to meet with. Don't even give you the time of day, not if you was to take a corkscrew to him.'

'Then let's go and talk to him now,' suggested Lees, his blue eyes alight with the fun of the challenge. 'I expect he's heard what's happened—maybe the shock will have loosened his tongue.'

'Unless he done it, sir—conscience might clamp upon his tongue faster nor it ever was before . . .'

But Lees, determined to enjoy himself, wouldn't listen. 'Mr Stockfish?' he called, as soon as they were decently near not to have to bellow in the presence of sudden death.

Stockfish stared, and brandished a spanner; but (though he made no acknowledgement of Lees's salute) said nothing. However, he didn't run away, which Lees took as a hopeful sign. 'Mr Stockfish, we're here to begin police inquiries into the unfortunate death of—'

'Ha!' cried Stockfish, so sudden and loud in his wrath that Perkes skidded to a halt and nearly fell flat in the mud. 'Pride and wickedness and haughty female sin was the cause of her downfall—as they should be for any female what thinks herself to know better nor a man, telling him his job, interfering in folks's lives when it ain't her business!' Turning his back on them, he gave some unidentified bit of the pump a hefty wallop with the spanner. At once, the whole vast contraption lurched into life with a thudding roar, so that there could be no possibility of saying anything further to the mechanical misogynist just now. Lees, with a shrug, nodded to Perkes to head for the main door.

Sheltered in the porch, with the cacophony of the pump partly muffled, Lees remarked, as Perkes tugged on the bell-pull: 'Very cheerful, wasn't he? Helpful, too . . .'

Perkes sounded puzzled. 'More words than I can rightly think I've ever heard him say, all at one time, so it was— he's not sorry, not Sampson Stockfish ain't!'

Before Lees had time to enlarge upon this, Gilbert Peck opened the door to them: a florid, middle-aged man radiating whisky fumes, and looking miserable.

'It's been such a shock,' he muttered, as they wiped their boots and changed into their shoes in the hall. 'Dreadful, simply dreadful! Who could dream that a birthday party— that it would end in—that this would happen?'

'Naturally it's been a shock,' agreed Lees, 'particularly to the person who discovered the—unfortunate lady.' And he coughed quickly. 'Now, the sooner we can sort out this business, the sooner life can return to normal—so perhaps you'd be kind enough to show me where she is? And I'd like to speak to whoever raised the alarm—'

'Oh, sir, it was me!' burst out Susan Grindstone, who'd sneaked through the green baize door into the hall and been making furtive signals to PC Perkes. 'Lying there under the table, all crumpled up and with her head bashed about, and the stick there as bold as you please beside her poor body —looked like a bundle of old clothes, so she did, but when my broom bumped into her I peeked underneath and, oh, sir! I couldn't help it, I gave such a squeak, I was mortal afeared of the sight, for my heart was going so fast I thought I'd be fainting away cold on the floor—only I didn't.'

'You rang me instead, didn't you, Susan?' frowned Perkes, attempting to stem his loved one's torrent of chatter. He formally introduced her to the Superintendent, confirmed what he could of her statement, and retreated to stand near the body, staring down at his boots and hoping he'd made no great error of procedure or protocol.

Lees was perfectly affable, and almost chatted back as he led Susan towards the oak table. 'You found her under here, you say?' He did not raise the anonymous white sheeting that covered the humped figure on the floor; kindly, he moved her to one side, so that she wouldn't have to look too closely. 'You didn't touch anything?'

'Not a thing!' swore Susan, miming her morning discovery for him with the broom, which still lay where she'd dropped it. 'Sweeping like this, I was, and then—oh, sir!'

'Quite so,' he smiled. 'And you tell me that Mr Goffe can confirm it—so how came the body to be moved?'

'It's my fault, I'm afraid.' Gilbert looked ghastly. 'When I heard the news, I couldn't believe—Dr Pickbone was here with me, and we pulled her out to see if there was anything we could do for her—and there wasn't . . .'

'Don't agonize about it,' Lees counselled. 'Clearly, she wasn't hit over the head under the table—she must have been moved there afterwards. But did either of you—any of you—touch this stick?'

'I don't think so . . . not that I remember . . . no, sir!' came from his enthralled audience.

'Well, until the forensic boys turn up, we can't hope to check for fingerprints or anything,' announced Lees, looking again at the swagger-stick. There were no stains, no hairs, no signs that it (presumably) had been used to kill the person beneath the sheet . . . the person he'd delayed too long in seeing. He took a deep breath, and grasped a corner of the sheet. 'The first thing, of course, is to identify the body—just so we know exactly where we are. Mr Peck, could you tell me, officially, who this dead woman is?'

'Her name is—was, I suppose I must say now—Jane Nightwork. She's—she was my aunt's nurse.'

Lees looked down at the black bruise upon the temple, the marks of battery across the neck. 'It appears to have been pretty quick,' he muttered. 'Let's hope she never felt it.'

'I—I think I'll leave you, if you don't mind,' Gilbert gasped, looking suddenly pale, and shaking.

'Yes, of course—how thoughtless of me,' replied Lees, eyeing him appraisingly. 'And, Miss Grindstone—maybe you could see about some good strong, sweet tea for Mr Peck—and for PC Perkes and me, if you'd be so kind? It was very cold on our journey here, and rather wet, too.'

The policemen were left alone in the hall with the body, to give it what examination they could, in the circumstances. 'She's definitely dead—looks to me as if he bashed her across the temple, probably with this swaggerstick (it fits the bruising easily enough, doesn't it?) and then chopped her across the neck. I wonder if that was necessary? If she turns out to have one of those eggshell-thin skulls the victims in detective stories always have, it was more like spite to do it . . . so then, I wonder why?'

'*I* wonder how long she's bin dead, sir.' PC Perkes was enchanted by this opportunity of working with the top brass, and was determined to prove himself. 'Mr Peck mentioned as how Dr Pickbone was here, didn't he?'

'Good man. Suppose we fetch him out of the dining-room to give us his advice? And then, I imagine I'll have to try a spot of solo investigation—we must keep the body under guard, you see, until the forensic lot arrive—photos and so on. I'll arrange with the fair Susan to have you supplied with blankets and hot tea—and could you ask Mr Peck, while you're fetching the doctor, if there's somewhere private we could use for an interview room?'

'And why,' demanded an irate voice from above their heads, 'don't you ask me, young man? It's *my* house, you know—so never mind that black sheep and his private rooms—if *I* say you can have a room, then a room you'll have, all right!'

'Mrs Keepdown,' mumbled Perkes, scuttling forward to help her down the stairs. Kate motioned him away.

'If your employer has told you to fetch Francis Pickbone, then that's what you should be doing—you certainly would if you worked for me! Go on, be off with you now!'

Perkes looked to Lees for permission, which was grinningly granted. 'Mrs Keepdown?' The Superintendent introduced himself, and assisted her down the final few steps. 'I've heard a great deal about you, but I'm sorry that I've come to meet you in such sad circumstances.'

Kate sniffed her opinion of the circumstances, even as her black eyes twinkled her appreciation of his courtesy. 'When you've lived as long as I have, young man, there isn't much that surprises you! I was ninety yesterday—d'you know that? And the next thing, here's this girl, dead, in my own house—murdered, they say—by one of *my* guests! No sense to any of it, is there? And all that silly Susan does is rush up the stairs bleating away about calling the police, and nobody seeing if *I* might want anything—no breakfast did I have, and nobody to help me get out of bed, either. When you're as old as I am, you don't have many pleasures left, you like everything to be easy for you . . . and I can't find my swagger-stick anywhere,' she ended, with a sigh. 'I'm not normally such a poor old cripple, you know!'

'So I understand, Mrs Keepdown,' Lees soothed her. 'But I'm afraid—about your stick . . .'

She followed his gaze to the sheeted shape on the floor, and the swagger-stick beside it. 'Oh, I see,' she nodded. 'So that's where it's got to, has it? Well, I don't suppose I'll want to use it again after this, somehow . . .'

'Kate, really, you shouldn't be out of bed!' scolded Dr Pickbone, reappearing beside PC Perkes, and so surprised to see her that, for an incautious moment, his apprehensions left him. 'Running about the house with nothing to support you—I mean, coming down the stairs without—'

One of her cackles broke into his embarrassed blustering. 'You don't have to fuss about me! I know perfectly well it was my stick they did it with—poor Keepdown, what would he have said about it all?' And she sighed, deeply melodramatic. 'A fine thing to happen . . . oh well, I'm ninety, after all. I suppose she was a good girl—good enough at her *job*, I mean . . . But I'm too tired to think about it properly now. Francis, I'll go and sit down, then they can send me some breakfast. And Susan shall find you a private room, Superintendent!'

Lees had to smile as he watched her, shaky but unshaken, being piloted away by Pickbone. 'She's every bit of what I heard, and then some,' he whispered to Perkes before giving him further instructions. 'When they made her, I'd say they broke the mould, all right!'

'And you'd be quite right,' echoed Dr Pickbone, emerging once more into the hall. 'Only one Kate Keepdown in this world—thank heavens!' But his chuckle, as he met Lees's reciprocal smile, seemed a little forced.

'Perhaps, Doctor, you'd give me an idea of time of death? We've guessed around midnight, but it might be helpful if you could narrow it down for us . . .'

Lees looked the other way as Pickbone busied himself with what skill he could muster, having few instruments and being himself, the Superintendent could tell, in a shocked state. Not as bad as Gilbert Peck—but certainly worse than Kate Keepdown, that indomitable old personage who claimed that old age left you surprised by nothing . . .

'It's hard to be sure, but my guess would be nearer one or two in the morning. Suppose we say between midnight and three a.m.—that won't be far wrong, I think.'

Lees dismissed him with thanks, then addressed PC Perkes. 'First, we must make a list of everyone who was in the house last night—do I take it that we're ruling out interference from burglars, or other nefarious intruders?'

'Yessir—unless it were one as didn't mind wetting his feet pretty bad. Besides, Susan (Miss Grindstone, that is) would swear to it as all the doors and windows was locked, same as usual, and I'd be inclined to believe her, sir.'

'Love is blind,' smiled Lees, so cheerfully that Perkes felt no insult on his lady's behalf. 'Step along to the kitchen, would you, and fetch your young woman and her pals to the dining-room, to join the others? I'd like to give 'em a pep-talk before I have to start proper investigating . . .'

He stared once more at Jane Nightwork, admiring the fair hair and delicate features revealed by the pulling-back of a sheet as white as her dead face. 'Poor girl,' he said, then covered her quickly as PC Perkes, trailing a small and noisy domestic caravan, came out of the kitchen and headed for the dining-room. Lees summoned him to a solitary guard duty, and made his own way along the hall to Kate's guests, and her servants—to his suspects.

'Good morning, ladies and gentlemen. I'm sure you know what's happened—that Miss Jane Nightwork has been killed. Someone took Mrs Keepdown's swagger-stick and battered her to death with it, concealing the body under the hall table where Miss Grindstone—' bowing towards a blushing Susan—'found her this morning. Now, I'm sure you're all just as anxious as I am to clear up this unhappy business quickly. The best help you can give is to answer every question as fully as you can—to tell me anything which might be of the slightest interest—and not, I repeat *not* to conceal things. I'll only find out in the end, so just think of all the unpleasantness you'd save by your cooperation . . .

'Dr Pickbone—' another bow—'tells me that she met her death some time between midnight and three this morning, so suppose we begin by your telling me where you all were then?' *But I'll bet a million that you'll swear black and blue you were tucked up nice and neat in your cosy little beds—same as me— oh well, that's life* . . . 'Incidentally, if you'd also tell me, each of you, at what time you last saw the deceased alive and well, it would be a great help.'

General murmurings confirmed his silent assumption of the sleeping-in-bed alibis—although Pickbone, Visor and Seely explained that they, being castaways, had slept downstairs, not up.

'But,' pointed out Pickbone, 'with all the exertion of shoving the car around, and the whisky we had to warm us, I for one was dead to the world—besides,' he hurried on with a wince at his unfortunate phrase, 'there was quite a storm last night, as well as that pump racketing away outside. If she'd been shot, poor girl, instead of—what happened, I'm not sure I would even have heard that.'

More general murmured confirmation: unsurprising, really. And nobody had seen her since about eleven, when they'd gone to their own beds . . .

'Yes,' Lees asked, 'can anyone throw any light on why she wasn't in *her* bed? Obviously, before she went downstairs she'd been ready for bed—she's wearing a dressing-gown over her underclothes, and her hair's loose—so does anyone know what might have disturbed her?'

What Kate told him spoke for them all. 'I went up to my room, after dinner, and she helped me to bed—but she went down again when Francis and Visor came back because of the flood, so of course she had to come to tell me all about the fuss—it's *my* house, after all, and besides, I'm a sick old woman. I might worry myself into a decline if I didn't know what was going on—everything in the house, I have to know!'

Lees responded to her black-eyed twinkle with a smile of his own, but sensed some unease in the room at her final few words. What was it about this lively old lady which seemed to disturb some of her guests—or her employees?

'What was she wearing when she came to your room for the last time—dressing-gown, or ordinary clothes?'

'Why, her uniform, as she always did. Very prim and proper she could be about *some* things, you know.'

'I see . . . and at what time did she leave you?'

'Oh dear . . .' She was deliberately vague. 'I don't see as well as I used to, you know—not after my cataract operation . . .' Marian scowled, Cicely hid a smile, and Pickbone frankly grinned at this artless remark. 'Anyway, my eyes get very tired, so late at night—I wouldn't have looked at the clock even if I *could* see it, in the dark.'

Lees noted the speaking looks as he pressed on, 'Did you see Miss Nightwork at any time during the night? Or hear her go downstairs, footsteps, anything like that?'

She hadn't; but Cicely spoke up, tentative, yet sure she should. 'I think I may have heard someone walking, rather fast, and not heavy enough for a man—coming from the stairs and going past our door—then I heard a door open, though I couldn't say which one. And I don't know what time it was, because I was almost asleep by then.'

'But it wasn't your sister?' Lees was studying the room plan previously drawn up by PC Perkes, with assistance from Susan and Alice. 'So, if it was a woman, you'd guess it was either Miss Nightwork or . . .'

The space was labelled simply *Miss P*, since nobody could spell it, and Alice refused to soil her lips by repeating it for Perkes to phoneticize. Lees thought she looked familiar to him, but couldn't yet place her.

'I assure you, it wasn't *me*,' snapped Perigenia, with a toss of her head. 'I dare say there are some people here who think I might have popped along to dear Gilbert's room for a little—chat, in the middle of the night—but I didn't! I've been insulted in this house quite enough already, thank you very much—I know when I'm not wanted!'

Lees observed Kate's pursed lips, Matthew's grin—and

Sir Bennet's uncomfortable wriggle, at her words. Gilbert
Peck was shooting dagger-like glances in her direction . . .

'So we'll assume that Miss Nightwork came upstairs
about eleven o'clock, and probably straight to your room,
Mrs Keepdown, to explain what was happening. Now, I
know you're not sure when she left—but have you any idea
of how long she stayed?' Kate hadn't—because when a
person got to her age, they didn't notice time very much,
except that it always went faster than it used to . . .

'Can you give me any idea of what you talked about—
anything apart from the floods, and your visitors?'

A crafty look crept into Kate's bright eye, and her plump
hands folded themselves primly on her lap. She remained
mutinously dumb, but glanced sideways at Mr Visor—who
sat fidgeting on his chair, and cleared his throat.

'I wonder, Superintendent, if I might have a word?'

'Use the library,' commanded Kate, with flashing eyes
and a triumphant toss of her head. 'Susan, light the fire!'

Lees seldom felt the cold, and was unwilling to give Mr
Visor the chance to change his mind. 'That shouldn't be
necessary, thank you, Mrs Keepdown—I hope I won't need
to have anyone in with me for too long. Besides, I'd hate to
give Miss Grindstone any extra work.'

'Extra?' The old lady was amused. 'It's what she's paid
for! But, all right, stay where you are, girl—or, better still
—be off and fetch me my breakfast!'

'If anyone has things they should be doing,' announced
Lees, 'please feel free to go about your business. I only ask
that you don't leave the house.'

William Visor followed him unhappily to the library, and
sat down on the high-backed seat in front of the mahogany
desk, while Lees leaned back in the imposing, buttoned,
red leather armchair which had been weighed down by
generations of studious, letter-writing Keepdowns and their
guests. He felt more like a bailiff or a debt-collector, however,
since Mr Visor looked thoroughly miserable, and kept clear-
ing his throat without managing to say anything at all.

Lees decided to help him out. 'You wanted a private word, sir—may I venture a guess? Something to do with the visit Miss Nightwork made downstairs? And do I infer that Mrs Keepdown knew about it?' Visor gulped, then nodded, still struggling to speak. 'The deceased was, perhaps, a close friend of yours—and the old lady disapproved?'

The solicitor laughed bitterly. 'I know what you seem to suggest, Mr Lees, but you are mistaken—Jane was not my mistress, although we indeed had a close relationship, of which Mrs Keepdown very strongly disapproved . . .' Then he related the sorry story of his marriage, his liaison with Jane's mother, his lifelong yet distant interest in the girl, and the reason for her presence in Swan House.

'But, surely—your daughter was clearly an excellent nurse, so why should Mrs Keepdown feel affronted by her personal family circumstances? Nowadays—'

Only violent emotion could have induced Mr Visor to interrupt. '*Nowadays* has nothing to do with the matter, Mr Lees. Mrs Keepdown is ninety, and most definitely of her own times —Victorian ladies were morally bound to condemn all such —ah, lapses, or irregularities of birth or behaviour, even unto the third and fourth generation. I assure you that she is quite adamant in her attitude—indeed, she was so irate when she recognized the likeness between us and guessed at our true relationship, that she formed the intention of removing her business affairs from my firm just as soon as—as soon as possible. She told me so . . .'

'And she's the type of old lady who keeps her word.' The Superintendent understood quite a lot now—except: 'Why did she take it into her head to tell your daughter all about it in the middle of the night?'

'Who knows how the minds of old ladies work?' countered Visor. 'Perhaps she saw it as a golden opportunity, since I would be under the same roof as poor Jane for the first time ever? The floods did that . . . Whatever her reasons, she broke the news to Jane, who was, naturally, distressed, and too shocked to sleep—she could not bear to wait until morning to speak to me . . . she came downstairs to find me, and—poor girl, poor girl!' He buried his face in his hands, and stifled a resounding groan.

Lees permitted a sympathetic pause before asking: 'What was your daughter's reaction to the story? How did she take your confirmation of what Mrs Keepdown had told her?'

The solicitor appreciated the distinction. 'Why, as to the news that I was her natural father, I would say that on balance it pleased her. You must remember that she had been accustomed to think of herself as a posthumous child —but the cruelly abrupt way Mrs Keepdown chose to break the true story to her upset her. She had rated me—although not her mother—for the, ah, immorality of the seduction— she said most forcefully that I was not to be trusted, and Jane is—was, I mean—a most loyal girl. And to be told that, once this birthday business was over—'

He caught himself up, and to Lees's inquiring look, continued, '—she would be dismissed, and without a reference! No doubt Mrs Keepdown fears the tainting influence of Visor blood . . . You will see, Mr Lees, that we had much to discuss, and small privacy in which to do so, despite the screen—the very presence of Pickbone was a constraint, and we dared not speak above a whisper. Jane asked for time to think, adjust her ideas towards myself—she left, saying that we must talk again in the morning—and I never saw her alive after that.'

'Can you give me any idea of when all this happened?' he was asked, after a further sympathetic pause. But he knew only that it had been at least an hour later than the time he and Dr Pickbone finally managed to settle themselves.

'If you two slept in the sitting-room, who slept here?' The library still bore witness to some anonymous tenant, in dishevelled blankets, and armchairs near the fire. Mr Visor eagerly seized on this, and elaborated upon the sleeping arrangements heartily—but it failed to work.

'You spoke of this birthday weekend in a way that makes

it sound rather—special, Mr Visor. May I guess again? Was this gathering of the clans anything to do with—Mrs Keepdown's decision to get round to making her Will at last?' And Lees blessed his Aunt Ellen, and her love of gossip.

Visor clearly thought it was telepathy: his jaw dropped, and he blinked. Yet he maintained sufficient professional poise to be able to say: 'I cannot feel this to be a proper question, Mr Lees. Mrs Keepdown may no longer wish me to deal with her affairs, but there must always remain the expected discretion of solicitor for client   '

'While you, sir, as a solicitor, must know better than most the importance of assisting the police as fully as you can in the pursuit of our inquiries,' snapped Lees. 'Come now, you understand perfectly that there is no question of *private and confidential* when murder is concerned—just as you must also understand that, unless it is germane to the case, we never disclose what we have been told . . .'

'Then why do you not make your inquiry of Mrs Keepdown?'

'What?' In one laughing moment, the stern Superintendent was gone; the blue eyes of Lees twinkled irresistibly across the desk, and Visor smiled even before he heard: 'She'd have my head on a plate if I should dare to try! And it isn't my job to go bullying old ladies, even a holy terror like this one—which is the only way I'd ever find anything out from her. You wouldn't really want me to go in fear of my life for the rest of my days, would you?'

Visor sighed, but knew he was beaten: that heartfelt and frank appeal had convinced him, as he had known must happen in the end. He explained the details of Kate's remarkable inheritance-by-judgement scheme, the way she had abandoned it without warning, and her unusual family structure—he even sketched out a rough genealogy to show how she stood regarding next of kin—'Or rather, the unhappy lack of them.'

'Now then!' cried Lees, excited. 'If anyone had killed the

old lady—only they didn't, I know—but am I right in thinking that her nieces would have gained by her death?'

'In monetary terms, that is correct. However, I for one would greatly have benefited had she died before what she knew had become public knowledge—as it is . . . Moreover, no attempt has been made on her life, has it? And, since she has now named Mr Peck as her heir (unexpected and improbable though it was)—a court might view it in the light of an *intent* to make such disposition of her inheritance, were she to die now intestate . . . it is a most interesting and stimulating point, Superintendent, but I trust that this is merely a question of academic interest?'

'It's such a gorgeous idea,' murmured Lees with regret. 'A rich old lady, a house full of people all after her cash—I do beg your pardon, Mr Visor. Such idle speculation on your client's murderability—very wrong, I know. But—just suppose . . .'

Visor saw the point, yet had to object. 'I consider it extremely unlikely that, even in the dark of the hall, anyone could mistake Mrs Keepdown's short and, ah, ample figure for Jane, who was tall, and graceful of build. Like her mother.'

'And yourself,' replied Lees, without really thinking—for a new idea was working its way through his subconscious. 'I wonder—if it might be a case of mistaken identity?'

'If Mrs Keepdown is running the slightest risk of harm, I consider it my duty, despite our difference of opinion, to go to her,' Visor quickly told him, glad of the excuse. 'And may I remind you to be careful, in future discussions of your theory? To suggest that somebody in this house is capable of murder—'

'But *that*,' said Lees softly, 'has already been proved.'

Dr Pickbone's interview began with a general chat about the medical aspects of the case, and, as it progressed, he lost more tension than Lees would have anticipated an innocent man to be suffering. Even when the matter of Jane's nocturnal visit to Visor was raised, his surprise was either genuine, or very well simulated.

'Good gracious! How extremely rash of them—suppose I'd woken up? Lucky for them I didn't—most embarrassing, to be playing peeping Tom, even like that.'

'Ah yes, Mr Visor mentioned his belief that *you* believed Miss Nightwork to be his mistress—an attractive young lady, wasn't she? But I assure you that you ran no risk of interrupting anything of that particular nature . . .'

Curiosity overcame caution. 'Then, if she wasn't Visor's mistress, she'd got something else on him—she was blackmailing him, depend on it! What other possible reason would she have for creeping about looking for him in the middle of the night, the way she did?'

'Interesting,' remarked Lees, after a pause. Pickbone was about to enlarge on his theory, when: 'Interesting that you should jump to the conclusion that she was blackmailing him. It's not immediately obvious as an alternative to a sexual connection between them—so do you, perhaps, have some personal reason for believing it?'

As Lees watched the struggle clear upon Pickbone's all-too-speaking countenance, he wondered if maybe the doctor hadn't hit on the solution, anyhow—Jane taxes Visor with her parentage, demands some legal recognition—financial recompense, perhaps—Visor is afraid of the subsequent scandal, and silences her . . . but no. Wouldn't he need to rid himself of the old lady, too? And, as he'd pointed out, nobody had tried to kill Kate Keepdown, had they?

Yet.

His thoughtful frown intimidated Pickbone enough to drag out the grim tale of the botched abortion, all those years ago in London: 'When I was young, and foolishly inclined to panic, Mr Lees—it was greatly exaggerated, you see—but, although Miss Nightwork knew about it, from the way she behaved towards me I could tell she would take it no further. Why, she only told Kate out of—well, professional duty, or conscience, or whatever you want to call it.'

'You mean that Mrs Keepdown also knows of this?'

'I'm pretty sure of it, from the way her manner to me has altered. She's a very sharp, very strict old lady—but neither she nor Nurse Nightwork said anything directly to me about the whole sorry business. So what use would it have been to me to murder the girl, with Kate still alive—if I believed they might spread the word about me? People forget, after a time—'

'And Mrs Keepdown is still alive, isn't she, Doctor?'

'I'm not sure I like your insinuations, Mr Lees,' Pickbone said slowly. The Superintendent shrugged.

'Observation, not insinuation, surely—as it's true! Mrs Keepdown *is* alive and well—and she's the other person who knows your guilty secret, isn't she?'

'Really, this is rubbish! In this day and age—'

'But Mrs Keepdown's not a product of this day and age, is she? More than Victorian in her outlook, from what I've been told—and they made them tough in those days.' He adroitly changed the subject, as Pickbone turned purple. 'But is she as tough as we suppose? How about her heart— if somebody had relied on the shock of all this business finishing her off, would they have been betting on a good thing?'

'I'd never thought of it like that. Of course, anything's possible—she's ninety, after all, and she's had one or two attacks that gave some cause for alarm—but no one with any sense could bank on her popping off to order, shock or no shock. She'll probably last for years yet—although there's always the chance she could go tomorrow.'

'How about her eyesight? I noticed, when we were talking about it in the other room . . .'

Pickbone actually found himself laughing, and regaled the Superintendent with a blow-by-blow account of the Great Cataract Row. 'Though I believe she'd die rather than admit it, her sight's as good now as it ever was! She just puts it on—the poor, helpless old lady with no sense of time! It's all Kate's excuse for paying no attention to anything which doesn't relate precisely and exclusively to her—and her hearing's fine as well—so don't let her fool you with her act, Mr Lees. Because she'll try anything, if she thinks she can get away with it!'

'Thanks for the warning,' he smiled. 'So her hearing and sight are perfectly good, are they? And yet she would die rather than admit it—an uncomfortable choice of words, I think, don't you? Let's hope she doesn't do that very thing, this weekend.'

And, as Pickbone found himself dismissed from the room, he wished he had used another phrase to describe Kate Keepdown. Somehow, it was too much like tempting Fate . . .

CHAPTER 12

Cicely still could remember nothing which would serve to settle, once and for all, whether it had indeed been Jane who pattered past the Hackets' door during the night.

'I was tired—I'd woken up early,' she explained with a blush, 'and everything was rather exciting yesterday— with the party, and the floods, and—and so on.'

'You didn't by any chance hear Miss Nightwork leave your aunt's room again—and go downstairs, perhaps?'

Cicely giggled. 'Oh, I'm quite sure I didn't—I had my pillow pulled over my head. Promise not to tell why?' she beseeched him, as he stared: surely she wasn't scared of ghosts, or burglars? 'Marian—my sister—she doesn't know, of course, but she snores. Isn't it dreadful? So very unlady-like—wouldn't Aunt Kate be shocked!'

'Your aunt's a great one for proper behaviour at all times, isn't she?' he responded with a smile. 'Does she get on well with your sister?' For he remembered the scathing look on Marian's face when Kate mentioned her eyesight, and Pickbone's account of the Cataract Row.

Cicely was quite open with him—too much so? A cover? 'She doesn't approve of Marian because she's not making some good man happy, Mr Lees,' and she contrived to blush once more. 'Neither am I, of course, but she thinks there's hope for me. But because Marian has a career—she's a teacher, and knows all about stocks and shares—Aunt Kate says she's not womanly enough. She says you have to give up everything for your man—' she went decidedly pink —'and Marian wouldn't want to do that. She's far too independent!'

'And your sister would have liked to be left your aunt's money to invest?' If she could be frank, so could he.

'Oh, I'm sure of it—she was simply furious when Auntie said she was leaving it all to Gilbert Peck. You see, he's not even a blood relation, and, besides—Marian thinks he's been two-faced about it all.' For the first time, she wore a worried look; but she recalled his homily upon the irrelevance of nothing, and the need to know everything. 'They'd —well, already talked about—certifying whether Aunt Kate was mentally capable, or something . . .'

Lees couldn't decide if she was really as sweet, honest and naive as she seemed. The deep sigh with which he paid sad tribute to his professional cynicism fluttered the leaves of his notebook, and he wondered if his promotion had done him more harm than good; he doodled a frisky little mouse on the open page in front of him, then found himself scoring prison bars across its face in thick, black lines.

Perigenia made an impressive entrance, coiling herself into a chair with such fluidity that at once he remembered a film clip someone from the Vice Squad had shown him.

'Miss Perigenia, would you mind letting me have your real name?' He turned to a clean page, and wound down the point of his propelling pencil. 'Or shall I try a guess? Jean Perrie, perhaps—or, say, Georgina Parry?'

'How clever and inventive you are, for a policeman,' she cooed. 'Unlike some . . . you'd make a good agent. But, no it isn't—and I never use it now. Must I really say?'

'It helps to keep our records straight—and I promise I won't tell anyone unless I have to.'

'Very well, then,' she sighed. 'It's Accost—Mary Accost. And I suppose, if you *did* let it out, with all the publicity there could be, nobody would know it was me . . .'

Was she glad of the promised anonymity, or not? It wasn't easy to tell. 'I'll see what can be done, Miss Perigenia—but for now, I have some questions for you . . .'

He was amazed by her subsequent candour: the relationship with Gilbert, the reason for her presence at Swan House, Gilbert's need for money, her determination to spoil things for him with his aunt because of his reunion with Jane—

'You mean that Mr Peck and the deceased already knew each other? Are you absolutely sure?'

Yes, she was, and not a bit surprised, either. 'He's a real sex-pot, so experienced, and so clever—at least, he is in *some* things—only, he didn't know what he was letting himself in for when he tangled with me! He even got her to drug me, so he could have his squalid one-night stand with her —what a stupid thing to do! No wonder he didn't want me to come here in the first place—but I wasn't going to let him get away with it. He tried to make out it was just a coincidence—ha, ha, ha!'

'Nevertheless, coincidences do happen.'

'Gilbert and that nurse was no coincidence—it must have been planned! I'd have her up for assault, if I could, for drugging me like that—well, it's what you'd expect from her sort. These frustrated, dedicated types go right over the top when they decide to let their hair down, and I guess she thought that one night with *him* was worth any amount of fuss afterwards—he always preferred blondes, you see, and he can certainly make a girl feel it was worth it!'

'You seem to have more animosity towards Mr Peck, and his disloyalty to you, than to the nurse—despite her rather unprofessional treatment of you?'

'Oh, I can understand *her*, poor lonely bitch. Gilbert is

the real rat, because he knew all along what he was doing
—and he didn't keep to the rules. Well, I hope I've cooked
his precious goose with dear Auntie now!'

He eyed her thoughtfully, admiring the artifice which had
kept her young, fresh and blonde, when it was some years
(he supposed) since she'd been any of them. She'd grown
up hard and mean, ready to fight for survival, hitting back
at anyone who got in her way—but . . . would she kill?
And . . .

'Miss Perigenia, would you stand up for a moment,
please?'

'What!' But she was so surprised, she did as he asked.

'Just wait like that, could you?' And ignoring her hip-
slung, insolent pose, he hurried into the hall, to come
back almost immediately with PC Perkes. They muttered
together behind her back, and Perkes, with a nod, walked
round the desk, and back to the door, staring at her the
whole time. He went out, closing the door, and Lees sat
down.

'I'm not a monkey in the zoo,' she snarled at him, 'to be
gawped at by everybody—what the hell's going on?'

'You'd better sit down—I'm going to give you rather a
shock. You see, you're a tall, slim blonde—and so was the
dead woman. And it's easy, in the dark, to be mistaken . . .'

It was a shock all right. 'You—you mean—Gilbert, or
even that silly little baronet—half sloshed, the pair of them
—they wouldn't see properly—this is terrible! If you're
right, he'll try again! I want to leave here—and I want
police protection!' Then she started to work herself up into
a fine panic. He tried to calm her (he'd hoped to provoke a
reaction, but never this vehement), but was afraid he might
do more harm than good.

'Perkes, just slip along to fetch the doctor, would you?
I don't think *I* can slap her face—oh, lord!'

With the appearance of Pickbone, Perigenia's audience
doubled, and so did her efforts. But the doctor had fewer
scruples than Lees, and boxed her briskly about the ears,

whereupon she shrieked and hiccuped herself into silence.

'This gets monotonous,' remarked Pickbone, leading her to the door. 'Every day since she's been here, you know—she's up and down like a rocket.'

'Drugs,' stated Lees, without query. 'She mentioned something of the sort herself, in an oblique way—'

'Oh, they love to tempt fate,' Pickbone assured him. 'But one day, she'll push her luck a bit too far!'

And Lees wondered if she had indeed done so last night.

That silly little baronet could hardly meet the Superintendent's eyes, casting his own down to his lap, where his hands wriggled and writhed. Lees guessed that part of Seely's misery was caused by his evident hangover: did he wonder if, in a drunken fit, he'd done in Jane Nightwork without being able to remember it now? But Perigenia had said . . .

'I trust you slept comfortably in here last night, Sir Bennet?' It seemed a harmless enough gambit, but Seely went red, and mumbled an inaudible reply. 'Were you disturbed at all—anyone moving about, floorboards creaking . . . ?'

'I was not,' he returned, as firmly as he could.

'Nothing at all—no blows, cries for help and so on?'

'I was—extremely tired, and I went straight to sleep.' There was defiance now behind the wispy moustache, and Sir Bennet raised his head with a purposeful stare.

He had to be shaken. 'Have you any idea why the actress Perigenia believes you may have a reason for wishing to kill her?' The gossip he'd heard had given Lees his own ideas, but it was gratifying to have them almost immediately confirmed. Instead of protesting ignorance, the baronet was struck dumb with shock, his pink-rimmed eyes popping as if someone had squeezed him by his skinny throat.

'She's expressed her apprehensions concerning your feelings towards her,' Lees pressed harder. 'Do I infer from your lack of denial that you do intend her some harm?'

Seely tried to rally, but it was too late. If he'd only been able to face breakfast, perhaps he might have had more willpower: as it was, Lees didn't have to use the if-you-don't-tell-me-I'll-find-out-from-someone-else tactics, for Sir Bennet spilled the lot, blushing brightly as he did so.

'My feelings got the better of me, I suppose,' he wound up his dismal narrative with a sigh. 'But she'd been so—so welcoming, and she was here as Peck's—guest . . .'

'So you assumed she'd be fair game?' Lees considered his embarrassment too deep to be a cover for something else—in any case, the baronet looked too stupid to have thought of such a timely strategem. 'Oh, in the circumstances, I'd say your—error of judgement was understandable.'

'It was realizing just how angry she was with Peck which encouraged me, you must see—not that I listen to servants' gossip, naturally, but when her behaviour towards him proved it—and there was no sign of hysterics, or threats, and she seemed so—so approachable, and friendly . . .'

'Have you any idea of *why* she was so angry with Mr Peck that you thought she'd be willing to cry on your shoulder? Did the gossip you didn't listen to tell you that?'

A broken man, Seely ignored the gentle mockery, replying at once. 'All I heard from Susan Grindstone was that there had been some sort of quarrel that morning between Peck and the—the lady under his protection. But neither of them discussed it with me, so I had no idea . . .'

'One last point,' Lees helped him again, pitying his poor opinion of himself made even poorer by enforced repetition. 'The lady is very famous in her own sphere—as an actress, I mean. You must have been intrigued to meet her—but, could you tell me what most attracted you about her?'

Suspicious at last, Seely dared to frown. 'Surely this is not the time for joking, Superintendent?'

'No joke, I promise you, Sir Bennet. Please tell me.'

'It's—her hair, I suppose,' he admitted at last. 'It's so fine and fair, but thick and wavy—almost like Jean Harlow, or Monroe—so blonde it's nearly white . . .'

And, in the dark, just as all cats appear grey—do all

blondes appear white? Sir Bennet didn't give him time to work this one out properly.

'That woman is a positive menace,' he felt sufficiently emboldened to remark, in the doorway. 'It wasn't just me she was flirting with—young Goffe as well, for one, and I assure you that Peck didn't take kindly to it. If *he* had hit her on the head, it would be no more than she deserved.'

So, naturally, Lees asked Mr Goffe to come along next.

'Can it be my politics that put me so far up the suspect-list?' grinned Matthew, settling himself on the chair and tilting it back on two legs. 'Revolutionary, radical, fan of euthanasia and so on—though I don't have the foggiest idea why anyone would want to, er, euthanase a harmless nurse —still, ask what you like. My life's an open book!'

'I'm only really interested in the pages you've written during your stay here, for the present, thanks. But, if you want me to pass your name along to MI5, I'm always willing to oblige—I like to encourage enthusiasm.'

'A policeman with a sense of humour!' marvelled Matthew. 'What a rare animal you are, Mr Lees—my heart quite warms to you. I just wish I could help you now, but . . .'

'When did you last see Miss Nightwork alive?'

'Elevenish, when we all went up to bed—she was out in the hall being argued at by the cook, about shifting furniture or something—but I didn't hang around to hear it all. That Shortcake woman's got a poisonous tongue on her, and I know she'd got her knife into the Nightwork all right.'

'Oh? Any idea why?'

'General gossip and kitchen spite, from what I heard them muttering yesterday in their den—resented her inter-fering in the running of the house, that sort of thing. Last night's little spat was about not airing blankets, I believe.'

'Anything deeper than ordinary ill-feeling, would you say? Any definite hostility expressed towards her?'

'All-round nastiness, but nothing of murderous intent at all—fascinating as a sidelight on human nature's more evil aspect, of course—but, unless one of 'em went sleepwalking, and worked it out of his system that way . . .'

'Let's hope not!' laughed Lees. 'I don't know that I can cope with that sort of crime—but, walking . . . *did* you hear anything of anyone prowling about last night?'

'She must have passed my door to get downstairs—but no, sorry, I never heard a thing.'

'So Miss Perigenia didn't come tapping on your door? If she'd expressed an interest in you, I might have thought—'

'Me, and anyone else in trousers!' Matthew instantly interposed. 'Gentlemen may prefer blondes, but blondes seem to have *no* preferences—or she doesn't, anyway. That poor girl wasn't a bit like her—though she must have had hidden depths, under all the starch and uniform . . .'

'And she wasn't wearing her uniform when she was killed, was she?' murmured Detective-Superintendent Lees.

If people had recently been quarrelling with the deceased, then Lees wanted to talk to them. Alice was first.

This she took as no more than her due, cooks being queens among kitchen staff. Consciousness of her image made her loud in outrage and shock, and it took some persuading for her to change her attitude—but, in the end, natural unpleasantness triumphed over the hypocritical mourning she'd managed to maintain so far.

But she added little to what he knew already from other interviews. Jane's interference was roundly condemned, with her wicked ways—disappointment on the part of Alice when Lees refused to ask her to enlarge upon Jane's midnight rendezvous with Gilbert Peck, for she merely confirmed Perigenia and was then led on to something else.

'Yet, despite this, Mrs Keepdown was prepared to make Mr Peck her heir, I believe—sinful though he was?'

'She was—though I'll never know why. I couldn't hardly credit it when Susan told us! And him behaving like that—in his aunt's own house, too, what's always bin so particular—but that nurse, one look at *her* and you saw soon enough as she was a proper little madam, underneath it all!'

Lees resolved to have another word with Susan. Whenever anything juicy was to be eavesdropped, Miss Grindstone was the one to do it . . . 'To come back to the nurse, Mrs Shortcake—you must have been one of the last people to see her alive, if you were making beds together—'

'I never touched her!' she broke in, alarmed. 'Not one finger did I set upon her sinful head, no matter how she may tell you all her lies about it—not one finger, I say!'

Nothing more could be coaxed from her. Lees was finding the different views of the dead woman quite fascinating—a blackmailer, a liar, a passionate, secretive personality; an interfering, primly bossy, well-trained nurse. The late, not really lamented, Jane Nightwork . . .

'Well now, Miss Grindstone, what can you tell me about Mr Peck's row with Miss Perigenia? I gather that you were near them at the time—most embarrassing for you.'

She was so surprised he knew she'd witnessed the tail end of the quarrel that at once she blurted it all out: how she was tidying various bedrooms when Marian rushed from Gilbert's room at the entrance of the actress, and the lively dialogue which ensued.

'Yelling and shouting, so she was, and him trying to shut her up—but would she—not her! *I've got friends, and I'll pay you back*, she says, *I'll tell everyone what you are and how you've cheated me!* Shocking, to hear a lady carrying on like that, though she's no proper lady, for all her fancy clothes, you can be sure of that.'

'I suppose everyone must have heard it all?'

'You know, it's a strange thing, for I was sure as missus would speak of it, what with her room being right opposite, but never one word did she say, and her normally as sharp as a needle against what ain't proper. And specially with the other one being her nurse, what had made *her* so angry —along of Miss Hacket, you see . . .'

Disentangling the pronouns, Lees learned how Susan 'accidentally overheard' Kate's momentous announcement

of her intent to make Gilbert her heir. Politely waiting
outside the door to clear away in the dining-room, she'd not
wished to intrude upon what was clearly a family occasion;
'so natural it was for me to mention in the kitchen what was
said, seeing as what concerns change in the family concerns
us as works for the family. Mrs Shortcake and her brother,
they've bin with the Keepdowns since they left school!'

'Have they, indeed?' It went part of the way to explaining
Alice's pronounced dislike of the dead nurse—part, but not
all. 'Her brother—that's Mr Hour, isn't it?'

'Oh yes, sir, they're twins.'

'And Hour is the butler. Did he also have cause not to be
on the friendliest of terms with Miss Nightwork? Did she
interfere with the way *he* ran things, too?'

Susan's sly, quick look and portentous silence confirmed
Lees in his desire to see Hour next. The butler was (for a
change) stone cold sober, and therefore truculent to the point
of only monosyllabic speech, and again the Superintendent
had to resort to shock tactics.

'I have been told that your sister was heard to make some
threats against Miss Nightwork. Is this true?'

Alice's twin turned purple, and his voice throbbed with
determined denial. 'Not threats, never—not Alice! Didn't
none of us like the nosey-parkering young besom, but we
knew as she'd not be with us for long, so didn't have no call
to go bothering with the books no matter what missus may
have asked her . . . We considered ourselves justified in the
wrathfulness of our words, you must know, but not even
Susan made no threats, stolen watch or no stolen watch.'

'What stolen watch?'

Hour's report of the lost-and-found timepiece added one
more name to the suspect-list, but did not (as her brother
had clearly hoped) remove either Alice's name, or his own.
For, whether or not Jane had known (or even thought)
anything to the detriment of the Swan House servants, their
position would not have been a happy one if, after Kate's
death, Mr Peck had installed her as mistress—that matter

of *bothering with the books* (whatever that meant), for instance . . .

But the Superintendent was finding motives, credible and not so likely, thick and furious all over the place. He'd have to calm down, and look for one simple, straightforward clue before he started accusing the entire household—thank heaven that (or so it seemed) only two blows had been struck, or else he might start imagining Swan House was the Orient Express.

Those blows—the swagger-stick—where had it come from? How had it left Kate Keepdown's custody?

She insisted on being treated just the same as everybody else, and enjoyed tremendously all the extra attention she got to ensure that egalitarian treatment: doors held open, anxious escorts, arms to lean upon, and comfortable chairs positioned exactly as she would wish. Once again, she took her rightful place at the centre of the universe . . .

'When did you last see your fa- your stick, Mrs Keepdown?'

It wasn't what she expected, but her denial of certainty sounded genuine—she'd been helped upstairs to bed, so it might have been left behind then, she couldn't be sure . . . and there was a challenging look in her bright black eyes. He had the overwhelming feeling that this old lady was indeed the key to the mystery, if only he could persuade her to tell him; but she wasn't going to make things easy for him, and he would have to ask the right questions.

'Did you hear Miss Nightwork go downstairs later on?'

'I didn't hear her moving about at all—last night,' she emphasized the final words with a portentous nod. Lees was not slow to take the hint.

'You knew of your nurse's, ah, liaison with your nephew?'

'He's no nephew of mine! But every family has its black sheep, and the Keepdowns have Gilbert Peck, with his nightclubs and gambling and drink and loose women—and more than enough of those, it seems! He brings one here, and flirts with another—even that Marian came in for some of his fine attentions, you know—though I could tell you quite a bit about *that*, if I wanted to.'

'I wish you would, Mrs Keepdown.'

She chuckled, and shook her head. 'Don't rush me, young man! At my age, somehow time doesn't seem so important —you like everything to stay just as it's always been. That's why Marian's going to get a shock, expecting young Cicely to go on housekeeping for her when she's finally found herself a man! Mind you, she'll have to be firm, no shilly-shallying, or she'll lose him—when a girl sees the man she wants, it has to be now or never. And Marian's the type to throw a spanner in the works, the unnatural creature! Dried up with jealousy, you see, and envying her sister that young Henry—she'll have to learn to cook and keep a house tidy by herself once they're married. But it'll be no more than she deserves for plotting, with that Gilbert—going to have a brain-doctor say I'm crazy! Maybe I won't leave my money to the Cats' Home after all—Cicely shall have it for a dowry. Now *that* should encourage her to run off with her Henry, all right!'

'But—I understood, from what everyone's said about yesterday evening—that you'd made Gilbert Peck your heir . . .'

'Ha! You don't want to pay too much attention to people, you know—most of 'em are fools! I only *said* I would— anybody can *say* what they please, it's a free country—but to let that black sheep have *my* money, to spend on his hanky-panky and wild ways—oh no! But why shouldn't a poor old woman like me have her bit of fun? It amused me to see what they all thought about me really, once they thought they weren't going to get anything out of me—that Marian looking for a loony-doctor to have me certified, and everyone with miserable faces—oh, I found out who my friends were, right enough, when I said I'd make Gilbert Peck my heir!'

CHAPTER 13

Gilbert had fortified himself yet again with whisky, and did not present the appearance of a successful lady-killer—but was he a killer indeed? It proved nothing that he was still one more person unable to meet the Superintendent's eyes . . .

'Mr Peck, your complicated love-life must have caused you a few problems this weekend. At least fifty per cent of the problem has conveniently vanished now, hasn't it?'

Gilbert's head jerked upright, and his eyes blazed. 'My morals are no concern of yours, Lees—and that's a pretty sick sort of comment, isn't it, from a policeman?'

'At least you don't pretend not to understand me—even though my statement might not have been a totally accurate assumption. Suppose you clarify a few points for me?'

It had been neatly achieved, and Gilbert knew it: bluster could never prevail now against that intent, inquiring blue gaze. Lees looked omnipotent—and omniscient. Damn him, for having talked to so many other people first!

'I knew Jane many years ago—there was a misunderstanding, and we lost touch. I had no idea she was my aunt's nurse—I ask you, is it a sensible thing to bring your current mistress to a house with one of your old flames in it?'

'Your meeting was pure—coincidence, then?'

'Of course it was—how many times must I say so!'

'Miss Perigenia,' said Lees smoothly, following on from Gilbert's exasperated tone, 'says that you tried to prevent her accompanying you here.'

Gilbert laughed bitterly. 'I'd hoped to get in well with Aunt Kate—an old lady, you see, and very strict—and how could I do that, turning up with a blonde floosie on my arm? But Peri has a fearful temper, real spite and viciousness— they tell me it could be drugs, but I don't know. She went for the old girl with a knife on Friday evening, and had to be tranquillized. It was when I—went in to see how she was, that I found out Jane was nursing here.'

'And you, ah, renewed old acquaintance?'

'I went to bed with her—is that what you wanted me to say? But why shouldn't I? She was a consenting adult, if you can use the phrase of normal heterosexuals these days —we were glad to meet up again, naturally.'

'But Miss Perigenia wasn't so glad when she found out?'

'What do you think—that she stood by and cheered and gave us her blessing? She was furious—and I couldn't get her to see that it was only a one-night stand. How could I afford to run two women, when I can barely keep my own head above water a lot of the time?'

'Miss Perigenia must make money from her films.'

'So she does, when she's filming. It's rather slack now, though it's supposed to pick up soon—so she must have known I'd go back with her to London, instead of staying here in the sticks! I need money, every bit as much as the next man!'

'And I understand you're going to get it, Mr Peck.'

'What? Oh—yes, Aunt Kate. You could have knocked me down with a feather when Jane told me what the old girl was going to say, and she *did*—but that was before . . . she's bound to change it now, the way Peri's been talking, and the whole house full of gossip. Kate's no dozy old fool —she can put two and two together, unfortunately.'

Lees was just about to remark upon this amazing ability to be reconciled thus glibly to losing a fortune, when the exact words he'd heard struck home. 'You say Miss Night-work had already told you that Mrs Keepdown would make you her heir—*before the announcement last night?*'

Gilbert could have kicked himself. Evidently, there had so far been no mention of that whispered, overheard talk at the foot of the stairs—and he'd had to let it slip! The thing to do now was dismiss it, as having no bearing on the case —the less he knew (or was believed to know) of Jane's own knowledge and thoughts when she died, the better.

'I think she may have said something of the sort, being in my aunt's confidence, you know, her nurse—but I'd no *real* expectations, and was as surprised as anyone else when she told us—I thought it was probably one of her teases.'

'Your aunt,' agreed Lees, 'is an unusual old lady. Would that be the reason you and Miss Marian Hacket planned to get her certified as unfit to dispose of her own property? I must say, she seems sane enough to me . . .'

He could learn nothing more from Gilbert—the man would do nothing except answer evasively, or pretend he didn't know. Maybe Marian Hacket would be more cooperative?

He felt he was well on the scent now, and began with the matter of her relationship with Gilbert; and Marian, that withered unwomanly spinster of Kate's condemnation, blushed. But from anger, not embarrassment, and she spoke out firmly.

'There has been some talk between us of querying my aunt's mental stability, her fitness to make a Will—which we both agreed was in doubt—until he changed his mind!'

'Only after she said she'd be leaving everything to him, I gather. Which would surely excuse him?'

'Bah! Mere expedient, crawling self-interest—he's too afraid of upsetting her! Now *I* have no such scruples—if she's capable of leaving her money away from her own family, to someone we all know she despises, then she *must* be mad! I intend to consult a psychiatrist as soon as I can.'

'Maybe she was only joking? Maybe she'll change her mind now there's been all this fuss . . .'

She shrugged it off. 'If she does—after saying it, in public, before witnesses—then it proves I'm right, that she needs proper care, someone to organize her affairs. Perhaps a form of trusteeship—'

'Between you and, I take it, Mr Peck—was that the idea to start with? Until he decided he didn't need to fight, that is—was that what you were discussing when Perigenia came to quarrel with him yesterday morning?'

Marian blinked, looked surprised, and nodded. 'Not that I can tell you much about any quarrelling—except that that woman's voice went right through my head—I was suffering from a migraine, and all I wanted was to be left alone. And that poor nurse brought something to help me—she had a true healing gift, and I sincerely hope that you find out who killed her, and deprived the world of her services!' Those grim grey eyes softened behind their spectacled wall, and, for one moment, Marian looked human. 'She relieved my pain, she sat up all night when my aunt had those feverish spells and her bad attacks, and she even looked after that flighty blonde female who created those hysterical and un-ladylike scenes . . . she didn't deserve to die, Mr Lees!'

With a sigh, she forced herself into the present. 'But at least she's been spared any more of Gilbert Peck's foul attentions. We all know his immoral ways—a lecher, and a weak-minded fool. As an ally, I'm well rid of him—and as a trustee for poor Aunt Kate, he'd be totally untrustworthy! Now, Cicely may be a bit soft, but, if she's going to marry Henry Pimpernell, he'll do just as well, if not better—he seems to have his head screwed on the right way, and he's far from giving the impression of being a weak-minded fool!'

He regarded her with surprise, mingled with admiration. Either it was a good act—or she was genuinely concerned for her aunt's well-being: she could have insisted upon pressing on with her plan by herself, and who could have withstood her? In her quiet way, she was as formidable as Kate Keepdown . . . formidable enough to murder? Annoyed with Gilbert Peck and ridding him of his lady-friend out of spite—only, making a mistake?

Lees laughed: it was too far-fetched. And yet, there had been something in what she said, something nobody else had mentioned, that for one instant had set him wondering . . .

Henry had gathered from Cicely that there was nothing to worry about, and was therefore quite unworried. Lees looked

at the young man across the desk, and sighed with relief—
that solemn, staid, respectable face was the very antidote to
flights of desperate fancy, so near the end of the book. Never
mind if no decent, credible suspect had yet appeared—stop
clutching at straws, and get back to some detection!

Henry denied all previous knowledge of Jane, but as most
other people had done so too, Lees was inclined to believe
him. And his story was much like the rest: deceased last
seen around eleven o'clock, no mysterious noises heard
during the night, no idea of what had happened until Susan
Grindstone started yelling the place down . . .

'Did you see much of Miss Nightwork during your visit
—in her professional capacity, or socially?'

'Hardly a thing. I probably wouldn't have noticed her in
any case, with my cousin Cicely's acquaintance to renew,
but, apart from last night (when she came in with my
great-aunt), she was always too busy looking after everyone
who wasn't well. Poor Marian with her migraine, for a start,
and that actress of Gilbert Peck's. The fool—fancy bringing
her to this house, and compounding the felony by seducing
the nurse! It'll serve him right if Aunt Kate *was* just joking,
and had no intention of making him her heir—it was all so
pointed, when you think of it—saying *unless anything happened
to make her change her mind,* and then asking like that for the
matches, and a candle—I·bet she's burned all four Wills by
now, and left it to the Cats' Home after all, just to surprise
everybody!'

'*What did you say?*' demanded Lees, and Henry jumped.

'What did I say? You mean—Aunt Kate didn't tell you?
But then, I suppose she wouldn't—though I would have
said that maybe Gilbert—but, no. And anyway, what's it
got to do with that poor nurse's death?'

Lees took a deep breath: and another. He tried to sound
calm, and reasonable, and persuasive . . . 'Do I deduce,
from what you've said, that your aunt has made four Wills
—and that Mr Peck knew about it? Four Wills—let me
guess—one each for the four of you . . . *did she?*'

For the first time, Henry looked discomforted. 'Surely, that must be Aunt Kate's personal business? I mean—I only found out about it by mistake . . .'

The Superintendent wormed it all out of him in the end. Henry's plastered arm had made him much slower in preparing for bed than the others; the bathroom was at the top of the stairs; he'd walked in slippers, quietly, to avoid waking anyone already asleep—and had overheard Gilbert, talking at the bottom of the stairs with Jane.

'Not everything they said, Mr Lees, but enough—my aunt has written, and signed, four Wills, and hidden them in her room. She was going to burn the three she didn't want, once she'd decided to name an heir. It's just the sort of trick she loves—I'm sure she thinks she means it, at the time— but it doesn't take much to change her mind. Gilbert, you see, and the nurse, probably don't know her as well as I do, so they'd be likely to believe every word . . .'

'Your aunt leads an exciting life, Mr Pimpernell. If any unscrupulous person had found out—'

'Yes, but nobody's murdered Aunt Kate, have they? And I doubt if anyone could even find those Wills—I don't think I could, and I only know that she once told me that there's a secret drawer in her bedroom. Nobody can find it—they made things well, in the old days! When she was young, she was apprenticed to an interior decorator, or whatever they called them then, in London—she knows a great deal about furniture and so on . . .'

With much to ponder, and a liking for fresh air, Lees decided that his final interview (with Sampson Stockfish) must take place, now that it had stopped raining, outside, by the pump, whose thudding still reverberated faintly through the walls in intermittent bursts.

'Keep an eye on things, Perkes,' he instructed, shrugging on his mackintosh again. 'And don't let anyone go upstairs —tell 'em it's in case of spoiling fingerprints, or the girl's last footsteps, or something.'

Stockfish was on pump-duty, spanners and oilcan to hand,

and a wary expression on his face as the tall Superintendent
approached. But Lees for some time said nothing, maintain-
ing a silence as serious as Sampson's own—thus proving
himself to be not only a man of authority, but of sense as
well—which two do not always go together.

'Interesting job,' remarked Lees at last, as the pump fell
quiet, and Stockfish dribbled a few drops of oil on a judder-
ing cog, and wiped it with a rag. 'I imagine you have a very
responsible position in the household?'

Since it was no idle curiosity, but a recognition of his
importance to Swan House, Stockfish was willing to reply.
'Find it hard to get along without me, th'old girl would—
same goes for 'em all, wenches and menfolk alike.'

Lees recalled the misogynist streak as he inquired: 'How
did you get on with the nurse? Mrs Shortcake and the others
don't seem to have thought much of her.'

'Interfered overmuch with them and theirs, so she did—
a young foreign wench has no call to do such, not being in
the house for ever as *we* are, knowing the ways of the place
—ah, but that's women for you.' He spat. 'Sinful too, she
was, or so I heard tell—though she spoke me fair enough
when I had to sign of them Wills for missus—but 'twas all
her cunning, d'you see, her sly way of hiding her wanton
passions. Prim and proper as they come, so she seemed—
but there have bin vastly differing tales about her since!
Like all women, when you consider 'em—missus was such
a rare one too, in her day, running off with another woman's
man—so did that nurse get her just deserts, and doubtless
missus will be up for *her* judgement, soon enough.'

'Yes, of course—she was ninety yesterday, wasn't she?'
But Lees found his heart wasn't in it—suddenly, he *knew*.
'She must trust you a great deal, letting you witness her
Will like that—as, naturally, she would do. Trust you, I
mean—she told you what it was, and so on?'

'Hadn't got no call to tell me—on account of it was me
as went into town and bought 'em all for her! A foolish
idea so it was, and tricksy—but that's just like her, and

doubt not but that she'll do plenty more before she goes.'

'Goes? Oh yes, ninety, of course . . . you could be out of a job then, I suppose. Will you retire?'

Stockfish spat again. 'As long as a man can work, so then he should, in honest labour—turn my hand to anything, I can—bit of gardening, carpenter and joiner, paint and decorate and fashion things tidy—'

'Really?' Lees's tone was one of delighted surprise. 'Then you're just the man I'm looking for! Tell me—our Crime Prevention people are pretty hot on burglaries, and I feel it's up to me to set an example, but I don't want to go to all the expense of a wall safe or anything—but if I had, say, a secret drawer in my bedroom—just for the important things, passport, insurance, savings books and so on—what would be the best place to put it?'

Experts love to expound: it flatters them. Sometimes it can be hard to stem the flow of simple (to them), baffling (to you) information—Lees listened, entranced, as Stockfish spoke of hidden springs, sliding panels, and false bottoms; of pivots, and balances, and knobs to be pushed or pulled; of hollow bedposts, and threaded spindles. But he got what he wanted, and returned, satisfied, to the house: where he addressed PC Perkes.

'If anyone comes out, don't tell 'em I'm back, please. I want to have a snoop upstairs—keep 'em away from me . . .'

The stairs, still swollen from the damp, didn't creak. *So that's how she managed it without anyone hearing—whole armies could do it without a sound, except for their boots!*

He opened Kate's door with a caution unnecessary in one whose orders have been obeyed. He didn't go in, but went on, after peering in, to Jane's room. Her door hardly made a sound. Her bed hadn't been slept in; the curtains were still tightly pulled together. He sighed, and opened the connecting door into Kate's room. It, too, didn't squeak.

The faint scent of rose-petal powder and lavender-water mingled with memories of physic and embrocation; the sun, pale but at last triumphant, danced through the windows upon tiny silver and golden motes. One faint ray was reflected from the age-spotted mirror on the dressing-table, and Lees went across to stare at his own image in the way so many people in detective stories must, when there's nobody about to notice them otherwise. This duty done, he began to snoop.

Of course it was the last drawer he investigated which proved to be the right one. He prodded, poked, and disconnected the false bottom—to gaze, enthralled, at what it concealed: several faded sepia photographs, and half-a-dozen folded pieces of paper, four of which were of heavier quality, and more finely written upon, than the others. He studied all six closely, sighed, and replaced everything as he had found it; looked quickly round the room, smiled at the candlestick and matches (unused) by Kate's bed, and went out.

PC Perkes was engaged in decorous flirtation with Susan as Lees came downstairs, but she melted away at once, and Perkes blushed.

'Never mind that now,' he was told. 'I'm just going to have a few words with everyone, so you might slip along to the end of the drive to see if the forensic gang are on the way yet—take Miss Susan with you for company, if you like. It's love that makes the world go round, isn't it?'

In the dumbstruck dining-room, every syllable he uttered fell like lead into the silence. Blank, deliberately calm faces turned towards him, listening; and nobody drew breath without wondering if their next might be as a prisoner.

'I'm sorry to have kept you waiting, ladies and gentlemen, but I hope it won't be for much longer. As soon as our forensic people arrive, things should be tidied up—because, you see, I believe I know who killed Miss Nightwork.'

There was a concerted gasp; Cicely gave a squeak, Marian stiffened, Henry patted his betrothed reassuringly on the shoulder, Gilbert scowled.

'Dr Pickbone—you'd agree, I think, that it would be a

good idea to spare Mrs Keepdown any unnecessary stress
and excitement?' For Lees had looked once, briefly, at Kate
—who alone hadn't moved as he made his announcement,
but sat with pale cheeks and a strained expression.

'I certainly do,' said the doctor. 'On top of the worry of
the broken leg and the operation, Swan House hasn't been
the most peaceful of places during this weekend—and it's
not good for a convalescent. No more sudden shocks, please
—if you'd explain things to her in private, I'll settle her in
bed afterwards. You shouldn't have come downstairs at all,
Kate, you realize—but I know it'll take more than anything
I can say to make you behave sensibly.'

They shuffled apprehensively to the library, ignoring the
shrouded white bundle on the floor in the shadows; and
Lees insisted that Pickbone should leave the pair of them to
talk over everything alone. 'You can trust me to break it to
her gently, you know,' he said, and had his way.

As he sat down beside her in her comfortable chair, she
twinkled one of her bright smiles up at him, and asked, 'So
am I to hear what you've got to say for yourself, young man?
Speak up, now—I want to know everything!'

'And so you shall, Mrs Keepdown. Although I wonder
just how much you already know that you haven't told
me?'

'And just why do you think—'

He raised an imperious hand. 'No, Mrs Keepdown, don't
let's get all hot and bothered. Suppose you simply listen to
what I'm going to say, and don't breathe a word until I've
finished? You can't always have it all your own way!

'Good,' he smiled, as she pouted at him, but nodded, and
primmed her lips. Above that tightly-closed mouth, those
deep-set eyes still sparkled, made blacker than ever now by
her pallor. 'Well, Mrs Keepdown, I've said that I think I
know who killed Miss Nightwork—and I think it was *you*.
I believe I know why, too—but how did *she* find out about
it? And what on earth am I going to do with an old lady
like you, up on a charge of murder?'

'Murder, indeed!' she snorted, forgetting her promise in the excitement of the moment. 'Ha!'

'Murder, indeed,' he replied. 'You had to keep her quiet, didn't you—you didn't want her spreading the story of your bigamy around, so you had to kill her.' Kate gasped, but yet said nothing to this charge. 'I suppose she found out on one of those occasions when you were feverish? You'd have been rambling, not guarding your tongue—if Jane was alone with you, she'd have worked it out from things you said. But she did nothing about it, being such a good nurse—because the sickbed is rather like the confessional—'

'Confessional, bah! Don't bring your popish talk here! Confessions and sins and all that nonsense—I'm glad she's dead, and I'd do it again tomorrow, if I had to!'

'Covering up one crime with another? Because bigamy is a crime too, you know—but of course you do! Otherwise you would never have needed to murder your nurse . . .'

She gave him her sweetest smile. 'You're a very clever young man. How did you find all this out?'

There was more than one way of answering her. Lees would take the oblique route, for the moment, to the truth —maybe later he would be more direct—and cruel . . .

'You're notoriously a very strict person, Mrs Keepdown, especially with people who lead an irregular life—so, when you announced that Mr Peck was to be your heir, naturally, it surprised everyone.'

'I told you—'

'Hush, now! Yes, I know what you *said*—but that was to me, afterwards, once you were safe. At the time, you *had* to mean it—or, at least, Jane Nightwork had to believe that you meant it. Because she'd blackmailed you into leaving Gilbert your money when you didn't really want to—disapproving of his lifestyle the way you've always done . . .

'And yet *your* life has its darker side, hasn't it? You didn't merely run off with another girl's fiancé, you risked scandal and the penalty of the law by marrying him when you had another husband, still living. But you believe that if the right man comes along, a girl should grab him at once, don't you? You said it about Cicely—yet you killed poor Jane, just for trying to hang on to *her* man. I'm sure only her feelings for your nephew could have changed her from a conscientious nurse to the blackmailer she became—but only to you, Mrs Keepdown. Nobody else would have known of your guilty secret—I think she'd have kept it from Peck —he'd believe she'd used her influence as your nurse to persuade you to bequeath him your estate.'

'As if I ever would! That black sheep, and my money—'

'But was it ever your money? Haven't you had your doubts about that? If you weren't legally married to Lucian Keepdown, all his estate must naturally pass to his sister's son, his next of kin—Gilbert Peck. Henry's only a grand-son, so he's too distantly related. And Jane spared you that embarrassment, didn't she? So long as you agreed to make Gilbert your heir, it was only putting to rights what should have happened years ago, when your husband died.'

She sighed, and caught her breath. 'My husband . . .'

'You made that announcement, and very pointedly asked for matches, and a candle—so that Jane could think you were going to burn the other three Wills. Oh yes, I know about them! Wills have to be bought—and witnessed . . .

'Then the floods prevented Mr Visor from leaving, and he had to stay the night. You'd already decided you had to do something, and this was too good a chance to miss—so, when Jane came to tell you what all the rumpus was, the extra guests and the emergency beds (wasn't she a courteous and considerate nurse?)—well, I bet you enjoyed telling her that she was a bastard, that one of the men downstairs was her father . . . Did you feel you were getting your revenge on her for having found out that you'd never been legally married to Mr Keepdown?'

There was a tired but knowing twinkle in her eyes, as she smiled with slow pride at her daring.

'Jane couldn't wait till morning to be sure—nobody with

that sort of thing hanging over them possibly could—which was what you relied on when you told her as you did, late at night, with the house quiet ... No one heard Jane Nightwork go downstairs, any more than they heard you going after her—you waited until she'd talked with her father, and knew the truth ... and then, once she'd come out of the sitting-room, into the hall ...'

For a moment, neither spoke. Then Kate sighed again and, reliving the memory in her dark eyes, relaxed upon her chair. Lees hated to press her, but he couldn't leave it like this: he *had* to be sure, even if it was an intolerable thought ...

'Mrs Keepdown—was it really your ninetieth birthday on October 29th—yesterday?'

'Of course it was!' she snapped, with a touch of her old fire. 'Didn't I have all my candles on my cake?'

'And—how old were you when you married, ah, what was his name, now?' He knew it quite well, but he would not distress her by letting her know he had pried among her well-documented secrets—too well documented, he feared, with their damning details, their conflicting dates ...

She tossed her head, and tried to sparkle, brazening out the secret she'd kept for so long. 'John Doit and I said we were both twenty-one—and so I was, a month or so later! What difference did a few weeks make, when he was in such a hurry to go to the Front? He wanted to be sure of me before he went to war—and how was I to know he'd be sent back the way he was, and not a hope of divorcing him, poor John! It was what my parents had been afraid of, you see, so that's why we ran away together to be married in London.'

'But—when you eloped with Lucian Keepdown, you really were twenty-one, weren't you?' Her silent nod was unnecessary: he knew it was so, from the spring-time date of that second certificate. Why had she kept the first? To have destroyed it would have freed her from the risk of inquiry—but women do strange things. Perhaps it seemed, to one of her moral, law-abiding nature, the proper course of action . . . He sighed again, for the pity of it all.

'Mrs Keepdown, I'm not sure, but I believe Jane Nightwork needn't have died—I don't think she was any threat to you at all, I'm afraid. If you married that first time under age, without your parents' consent, then I don't know if you were ever legally married to John Doit at all. Your first, and only, marriage was probably to Lucian Keepdown . . .'

'*What?*' cried Kate, turning white, her face twisting with rage. She closed her eyes in shock, and fell back upon her chair, her plump hands clenched in fury. After a long, calculating pause, Lees cleared his throat, and continued:

'Poor Jane was probably a kindly person, as blackmailers go—but I think you'd prefer to leave the money, say, to Henry and Cicely, since everyone seems to think they'll make a match of it—you simply hate being told what to do, don't you? So Jane Nightwork had to die . . .

'I wonder what was wrong with John, that you let him go home to Staffordshire alone? Shell-shock—paralysis—' He moved uncomfortably on his chair. 'Something pretty horrid, I think—and did Lucian Keepdown ever know? I wonder . . .' He leaned forward, and laid his hand gently on the two plump folded ones resting now, so very still, in the old lady's lap. 'I wonder—but I suppose I'll never know now . . .'

He straightened up, stretched himself, and went to the door. 'Dr Pickbone, could you come here, please? I rather think that Mrs Keepdown's had a heart attack.'

'Why the devil didn't you call me sooner?' snapped Pickbone, who could see at once that it was too late. 'I didn't think she looked all that well when I left you—but how long was she bad, for heaven's sake? I thought policemen were meant to be trained observers!'

'It seemed the best thing that could happen, in the circumstances,' Lees said slowly. 'You see—it was Mrs Keepdown who committed the murder.'

'*Kate* killed that nurse? Impossible! Why would she—ah,

wait! She found out about Peck, and was disgusted at the idea of another loose woman in the house—and one who'd been looking after her, to boot.'

'I expect that's the reason.' It would serve as well as any other; Lees felt reluctant admiration for the stout-hearted old lady who had defied convention in so many ways, and for so long. 'I'm told she was a very strict old person.'

'She was indeed—but to leave her money to Peck, as she did . . . she certainly wasn't mad, no matter what Miss Hacket likes to think—but she was always full of surprises. I dare say she'd have changed that Will, if she'd had time.'

'You know, she told me all that was just her notion of a joke?' Lees had made up his mind as the other talked— had weighed Gilbert's wasteful, unsavoury life against the happiness of Cicely and Henry, and Marian's gentler side which she could afford to show to few. 'I don't believe,' he told the doctor firmly, 'that she ever really made that Will —so I expect Mr Visor will tell us that those nieces of hers end up sharing the lot, as her next of kin.' He'd convinced even himself, so fair a solution did it sound; and, looking down at the plump, peaceful body, he remembered the candle and the unused matches—in Kate's bedroom . . .

He thrust his hands into his pockets. 'Oh, damn! Must have left my pencil upstairs—taking some measurements in the corridor—better go and fetch it. You don't need me for the moment, do you? So would you excuse me?'

As he made his way to the foot of the stairs, a burst of hearty conversation in the front porch told him that, once all the excitement was over, the forensic boys had arrived. But he did not stop to greet them, nor did he look back as he hurried purposefully up the stairs. What he had to do, he was sure, would not take long; and he was also sure that the sparkling eyes of Kate Keepdown would be watching him mischievously, content at last.